# Trif and T

A story of a dreadfully delightful
adoring and tormented parents, relations, and friends

John Habberton

**Alpha Editions**

This edition published in 2024

ISBN : 9789362090737

Design and Setting By
**Alpha Editions**
www.alphaedis.com
Email - info@alphaedis.com

As per information held with us this book is in Public Domain.
This book is a reproduction of an important historical work. Alpha Editions uses the best technology to reproduce historical work in the same manner it was first published to preserve its original nature. Any marks or number seen are left intentionally to preserve its true form.

# Contents

CHAPTER I. A BABE IN THE HOUSE IS A WELL-SPRING OF PLEASURE. ............................................................................ - 1 -
CHAPTER II. A TRANSACTION IN COTTON. ...................... - 7 -
CHAPTER III. UNAPPRECIATED. ......................................... - 13 -
CHAPTER IV. IN CHARGE OF EACH OTHER. .................... - 19 -
CHAPTER V. A SURPRISE. ..................................................... - 25 -
CHAPTER VI. ALL BY CHANCE. ........................................... - 32 -
CHAPTER VII. MORE REVELATIONS. ................................. - 38 -
CHAPTER VIII. A SNATCH AT TIME'S FORELOCK. ......... - 44 -
CHAPTER IX. MISPLACED CONFIDENCE. ......................... - 50 -
CHAPTER X. A SCRAP OF PAPER. ...................................... - 55 -
CHAPTER XI. OFF THE SCENT. ............................................ - 60 -
CHAPTER XII. THE SEARCH PARTY. .................................. - 66 -
CHAPTER XIII. A PLAN OF CAMPAIGN. ............................ - 71 -
CHAPTER XIV. THE COURSE OF TRUE LOVE. ................. - 76 -
CHAPTER XV. THE UNEXPECTED. ..................................... - 81 -
CHAPTER XVI. COWARDS BOTH. ....................................... - 87 -
CHAPTER XVII. THE COURAGE OF JOY. ........................... - 92 -
CHAPTER XVIII THE WOOING O' IT. .................................. - 98 -
CHAPTER XIX. THE MISSING GUEST. ............................... - 103 -
CHAPTER XX. A BLISSFUL WEEK. ..................................... - 108 -
CHAPTER XXI. APRIL SHOWERS ....................................... - 113 -
CHAPTER XXII. "THEY TAKE NO NOTE OF TIME." ........ - 118 -
CHAPTER XXIII. "BEYOND THE DREAM OF AVARICE." ................................................................................ - 123 -
CHAPTER XXIV. TRICKS UPON TRIXY. ............................ - 128 -

CHAPTER XXV. THREE BLIND MICE..................................- 133 -
CHAPTER XXVI. THE OTHER COUPLE............................- 138 -
CHAPTER XXVII. THREE DAYS GRACE..........................- 144 -
CHAPTER XXVIII. THAT SURPRISE. ................................- 149 -

# CHAPTER I.
## A BABE IN THE HOUSE IS A WELL-SPRING OF PLEASURE.

TRIXY was not a babe, for she had passed her seventh birthday and was as wise and irrepressible as the only child of a loving father and mother usually becomes. Her parents and relations continued to allude to her as "the baby," and they might still be doing so had not certain of her deeds checked them, and compelled them to restrict themselves to her rightful name, which was Beatrice, and to her nickname, which was Trixy.

Trif was Trixy's mother, and did not entirely approve of the name by which she was oftenest addressed, for "Trif" seemed to imply something trifling, while the real Trif was a young matron as handsome and proud as Diana, and as good and earnest as the saintly Roman woman Tryphosa, for whom she was named. (All this must be true, because Trif's husband, Phil Highwood, said so and continues to say it.)

Whether she laughed or wept, dressed or dusted, joked or prayed, Trif did it with all her might; so it was not strange that her little daughter was a very active and earnest creature from the instant at which she first opened her baby lips to announce her appearance upon the earthly stage.

Besides, Trixy's father was one of the conscientious and nervous fellows who are always wondering what to do next, always anxious to do exactly what is right, always trying to do friendly services to other people, and frequently blundering horribly in the attempt; so there was double reason for what Trif called "dear Trixy's peculiarities" and other people alluded to as "that child's awful doings."

Trif and Trixy lived far up town on the west side of New York. The husband of the one and the father of the other lived there too, although he is of minor consequence in this veracious narrative, for the neighbors and tradesmen knew him best as "that little terror's father," or "Mrs. Highwood's husband," and he was modest enough and proud enough to be satisfied to be known in this way.

With the family lived Trif's sister, Tryphena Wardlow, known best to her friends as Fenie—a charming and exuberant girl who thought her sister Trif the most perfect woman alive, was sure that Trixy was the embodiment of all the baby angels in heaven, and declared that she never, never, never would think of marrying until some man as simply perfect as her brother-in-law, Phil Highwood, should ask her, and as that seemed impossible she had determined, at the mature age of twenty years, to remain single forever, yet never become that dreadful creature called "an old maid."

Fenie had no lack of suitors, old and young, for all men like handsome girls who are also good, merry and accomplished; besides common report had it that Fenie and her sister drew between them five thousand dollars a year from the estate of their New England parents. Common report had set the figure about ten times too high, but never took the trouble to correct the mistake, so Fenie was the most attractive young woman of the vicinity, and many were the times when a merry evening which had been planned by Phil, Trif, Fenie, and Trixy, was spoiled by the appearance of some male visitor who had to be treated civilly, and who couldn't tear himself away from the witchery of Fenie's face and voice.

There was one young man, Harry Trewman, whom Fenie seemed rather to like, and whom Trif and Phil, with their larger knowledge of human nature, wished their sister could like still more, for he was intelligent, modest, and seemed to have many virtues and no vices. They talked much about him when they were alone—alone except for Trixy, who was always so competent to amuse herself and to be absorbed by her books and dolls and her own thoughts that she seemed deaf to anything that was being said, for it generally took half a dozen separate and distinct remarks to make her change her dress, or wash her hands, or go to bed.

The doorbell rang one evening while the family still lingered at the supper table, and the servant brought a card to Fenie.

"Oh, dear!" exclaimed the girl with a pout. "Here comes Harry Trewman, just as we were going to have a jolly game of parchesi with the baby. I do think that callers might remain at home on stormy nights, when a girl hasn't taken the pains to dress for company. That young man needs a lesson. He has sisters and they ought to teach him that ladies don't expect calls on stormy nights."

"It won't take you long to change your dress, dear," suggested Trif.

"No, but—"

"'Be not unmindful to entertain strangers, for thereby some have entertained angels unawares,'" quoted Phil, as he quartered a second orange for Trixy.

"Angels—umph!" exclaimed Fenie. "Harry Trewman doesn't resemble any angel of whom I ever saw a picture. He's no stranger either, goodness knows; he's been here at least once a week for a long time. You shouldn't ever quote Scripture, Phil, unless the application is entirely correct."

"Very well, then; 'Flee from the wrath to come.' Nothing makes Trif so provoked as delay in greeting a visitor."

"Poor little Trixy. Her game will have to be put off," murmured Fenie as she rose from the table and kissed her niece.

"Never mind me," said Trixy, from behind a kiss and a mouthful of orange. "The game will keep, but Mr. Trewman won't, if you don't be more careful."

"Won't keep?" exclaimed Fenie, with a frown at the child and a suspicious glance at the remainder of the family.

"Trixy!" exclaimed Trif in her most severe tone, while Phil put another section of orange into the child's mouth and his hand over her lips, while Trif continued:

"Go along, Fenie. Change your dress quickly; I'll run up stairs and help you."

"And I," said Trixy, after a struggle with the orange and her father's hand, "I'll entertain Mr. Trewman till you come down."

Three adult smiles were slyly exchanged as the child assumed an air of importance, tumbled out of her high-chair and started toward the parlor, while her mother and aunt slipped up the back stairway and Phil buried his face in the evening paper.

"Good evenin', Harry," said the little maid, as she bounced into the parlor.

"Oh, Trixy!" exclaimed the young man rising in haste. "How do you do, little girl? I'm very much obliged to you for calling me Harry. It sounds as if you rather liked me."

"So I do," replied Trixy. "I s'pose I ought to have said 'Mr. Trewman,' but papa and mamma and Aunt Fee always calls you 'Harry' when they talk about you, so I said it without thinkin'."

"Oh, they do, eh?" Mr. Trewman's clear complexion flushed pleasurably and his moustache was twirled thoughtfully. If the family talked of him familiarly, there seemed special reason for him to hope.

"Yes, they do it lots. I get sick of it sometimes, 'cause I want to ask 'em somethin', and mamma says I mustn't ever interrupt grown people when they're talkin', so I can't ask it, and afterward maybe I forget what I was going to ask, and that bothers me like ev'rythin'."

"You poor little sufferer!" exclaimed the young man. "I ought to do something very nice for you, to make amends for causing you so much trouble. What kind of candy do you most like?—or mayn't I bring you a new doll?"

"Papa and mamma don't like me to eat candy," said Trixy with a sigh. "They say it's bad for my 'gestion. Have you got a 'gestion?"

The young man admitted that he had, but he hastily reverted to dolls as a more appropriate topic of conversation. Trixy looked troubled and finally said:

"Oh, dear! Something always goes wrong. I need a new baby doll awfully, for the kitten bit the head off of my littlest one, but, you see, papa and mamma says it isn't proper for young ladies to accept presents from gentlemen."

"Oh, I see—I beg a thousand pardons," Trewman gravely replied. "But would you object to my asking your parents' permission to give you a new doll—the finest one that I can find?"

"Do it—quick!" exclaimed Trixy, her eyes dancing and her hands clapping gleefully. "I don't think, though," she continued, after a moment or two of thought, "that I ought to take somethin' for nothin', for papa says that folks who do that are real mean."

"Something for nothing? Why, you dear little bundle of conscience, I'm to give you the doll in part payment for the trouble I have given you. Don't you remember?"

"Oh, yes! To—be—sure. Well, I forget my troubles as soon as I tell 'm, so—so you don't owe me anything."

Trixy looked sad as the promised doll began to disappear from her mental vision, so the young man said quickly:

"You must have the doll, now that we've talked about it, and so that I mayn't lose the pleasure of giving it to you. You can give me something for it, if you like—for instance, give me a penny, to wear on my watch-chain."

"I'll tell you what," exclaimed Trixy, her face suddenly brightening. "I'll give you a lesson for it. You like lessons, don't you—I like 'em—like all I can get, and I've got one for you that Aunt Fee says you need, so I'm sure you'll like it, 'cause ev'rybody likes what they need, don't they?"

The young men admitted that they ought, if they didn't, but his face quickly became grave, and he looked furtively toward the door through which Fenie would appear, as he whispered:

"Tell it to me—quickly."

"Well, it ain't a very big lesson, but you needn't give me a very big doll. Let me see—what was that lesson she said you needed? Oh, I remember: she said that young men ought to know better than to go calling on stormy nights, when ladies don't dress up and be ready to see company. She said you needed a lesson about it, and you had sisters, and they ought to teach it to you. Mebbe, though, your sisters don't like to give lessons?"

"They're not as active at it as they might be," replied the man as he arose hastily and took from his coat pocket a small package. "But—er—perhaps I am not as much to blame as I seem. I dropped in to leave a book which your Aunt Fee wished to read but couldn't find, and I promised to get it for her. I might have left it at the door, but I was thinking very hard at the time about—about a person in whom I am greatly interested, so I managed to——"

"Oh, do you do that?" asked Trixy, following the young man, who was moving rapidly toward the front door.

"Do what?"

"Why, think of one thing while you ought to be doing some other thing? 'Cause if you do, you're just like me."

"Bless you, my child," said Trewman, as he opened the outer door, "I do it all the while. Indeed, no matter what I am doing nowadays, my mind is full of another subject."

"Dear me. What a nice subject it must be!"

"So it is;—the very nicest subject in the world."

"Oh! What is it?"

"I can't tell you now. Good-night!"

"Will you tell me some other time?"

"Yes, yes—that is, I hope I may."

Five minutes later, when Miss Tryphena Wardlow descended to the parlor she found only Trixy, who was rocking ecstatically in her own little chair and thinking of the doll to come.

"Where's Mr. Trewman?" asked the young woman.

"He's gone. He left this book for you, but he took his lesson with him."

"Lesson? What lesson?"

"Why, the one you said he needed. I gave it to him, and he's goin' to give me a doll for it."

Fenie looked puzzled for a moment; then her face became very red and she exclaimed:

"You dreadful child! Do you really mean that you have repeated to Harry Trewman the———"

Fenie stopped abruptly, darted to the foot of the stairs, shouted "Trif!" dashed through the hall to the dining room, and exclaimed, "Phil, come into the parlor—this instant." In a moment a mystified couple was staring at a young woman whose beauty was enhanced by a great flush of indignation; they also saw a tearful little girl who seemed to be trying to shrink into nothingness.

It took an hour of scolding, and petting, and warning, and kissing to prepare Trixy for bed, but when the child was finally disposed of Phil drawled:

"If you girls don't want things repeated by that child you mustn't say them in her hearing."

"But she never seems to notice what is said," explained Fenie.

"Umph! Neither does a phonograph cylinder, but it gets them all the same."

"All this talk about Trixy doesn't make our position toward Harry Trewman any the less awkward," said Trif gravely.

"Oh, bother Harry Trewman," exclaimed Fenie; but there was a look in her face which compelled Phil to glance slyly at his wife, and Trif to respond with a merry twinkle of her eyes.

---

# CHAPTER II.
## A TRANSACTION IN COTTON.

THE week that followed the Trixy-Trewman incident was a trying one to Trif. Her sister Fenie, although an intelligent and well-educated young woman who could talk well on many subjects, and whose interests were generally as broad as those of a clever young woman should be, would converse about nothing but the dreadful position in which Trixy had placed her toward a young man whom she cared no more for than for old Father Adam—indeed, not as much, for Adam was regarded by all good people of New England extraction as a member of the family, although somewhat remotely removed.

As for Trif, she had no patience with a girl who did not know her own mind. When she had first met Phil Highwood, nearly ten years before, she knew at once what to think of him, and she had never changed her mind. Neither had she thought it necessary to talk of him to the exclusion of everything and everybody else—not at least until she had been married to him and before Trixy made her appearance as the eighth wonder of the world and the most important creature ever born.

It would never do, she argued, to betray her feelings to and about her sister, for she had determined to have Harry Trewman for a brother-in-law, and her husband loyally supported her in her decision. But what was to be done?

Upon one thing she and her sister were resolved, and one morning after breakfast the couple called upon Phil to witness their resolution, which was that they would never again say in Trixy's hearing anything which could make mischief by being repeated. Phil listened with a smile so provoking that Fenie called him perfectly horrid, while Trif playfully but vigorously boxed his ears.

"Oh, you'll keep that resolution," Phil admitted. "I've no doubt whatever that both of you will live up to it—while the dear child is asleep, but if either of you blessed women think that you're going to leave anything unsaid that you want to say while you're together you're dangerously mistaken. You've been sisters and chums too long to hold your tongues at home."

"I flatter myself," said Trif loftily, while Fenie pouted exuberantly, "that we have sense enough to make each other understand what we have to say, and at the same time keep the child from knowing what we are talking about."

"Women aren't like men," added Fenie. "It isn't always necessary for them to talk to make themselves understood. Trif has told me thousands of things with her eyes, without saying a word."

"She certainly has a remarkable faculty at that sort of thing," said Phil, with a gentle pinch at his wife's cheek. "She often conversed with me across the entire width of a crowded room—just as you'll probably do, Fenie dear, when the proper man appears. At the present time, however, there's no sign that either of you will let your tongues suffer through lack of exercise."

"Trif," said Fenie, "isn't it about time for your husband to be on his way to his office? I'm sure his employers will complain of him for being late."

When Phil had departed, the two women, to make assurance doubly sure, called Trixy and gave a full hour of cautions against repeating anything whatever that she might chance to overhear in the house. She was reminded that she was mamma's and auntie's little lady, and that ladies never repeat what is said in the home circle, and that nobody liked tale-bearers, and that, although Harry Trewman was not of the slightest consequence—Fenie was elaborately explicit on this point—some dear friend of the family might be greatly offended by hearing something which was said only in fun.

Trixy listened attentively and promised profusely; then she retired to her doll's nursery to have a long season of thought over all that had been said. Fenie often worried about the habits of the child, for dreaming was more to her own taste, but Trif said that Trixy's way was entirely natural and proper; she had exactly the same manner when she was a little girl; besides, according to Phil's parents, the child's father had done much retiring for thought in his youthful days.

But Trixy had much besides thinking to do. She felt greatly mortified at having made any trouble, and the less there seemed to be of the trouble, according to her Aunt Fee, the more of it there was—according to Trif. She reverted to the subject, again and again, asking numberless questions at unexpected times, generally with the result of bringing a blush to Fenie's face. When Trif asked her husband what it could be that made the child so curious, despite all that had been done to belittle Harry Trewman in connection with the incident, Phil's only reply was:

"There's an old saying to the point—'You can't fool a child or a dog.'"

Meanwhile Trixy went on thinking, and one day she came to her mother with a confession.

"You see, mamma, I thought about it a lot, and I thought the best way not to repeat things was not to hear 'em, so I made up my mind that I wouldn't listen any more to anything that wasn't said right straight to me."

"Sensible little girl," exclaimed Trif, showing her approval further by a shower of caresses and kisses.

"Oh," said Trixy, trying to escape, "but you don't know how bad I am. Since I made up my mind to stop hearing things I've heard more of them than ever."

"You poor little darling," exclaimed Trif, snatching the child into her arms, "you must stop tormenting yourself in that manner. Stop thinking about it, dear. Listen when you like, and when you don't. Perhaps that will cure you."

"Oh, I know a better way than that," said Trixy, perching herself upon her mother's knee, and looking up with the expression of a cherub. "You remember that time when I had the earache and you put cotton, with smelly stuff on it, in my ears? Well, I couldn't hear a thing then. Now, I think———"

"Be quiet, dear," exclaimed Trif. "You talk as if you were some dreadful creature from somewhere, instead of mamma's darling, sweet, good little daughter."

A morning call put an end to the interview, but a few hours later, while Trif was sewing busily and Fenie was talking volubly and aimlessly about Harry Trewman, a light step was heard in the room, and Fenie dropped her subject for a moment, and exclaimed:

"Tryphosa Wardlow Highwood, will you look at your daughter—this instant?"

Trixy was evidently expecting to be looked at, and was pleased at the effect of her appearance. Over each ear was a great dark ball or wad of something, her mother could not imagine what, until examination showed that the outside of each was a rubber tobacco pouch, two or three of which Phil had discarded when he gave up smoking pipes. Inside of each was a mass of raw cotton, and the mouth of each bag was tied tightly around a juvenile ear.

"I can't hear hardly a thing," shouted Trixy. "A little bit of cotton in each ear didn't make much difference, but a whole lot on the outside made lots, and the bags made more, beside keeping the cotton on. Now go on talkin' all you like; I'm goin' to read."

"She shan't wear those dreadful things," exclaimed Fenie, untying the bags, despite Trixy's remonstrances. "She shan't keep cotton in her ears, either. The idea of the darling little thing being———"

"Let her have her way a little while," said Trif. "It will amuse her, without harming any one else. Besides, you may accidentally mention Harry Trewman in the course of the afternoon, and———"

There must have been a note of sarcasm in Trif's voice, for Fenie retorted sharply:

"Tryphosa, this is your house, and if you dislike that young man so much that you object to the child hearing the sound of his name, why I———"

"Fenie! Fenie, dear!" interrupted Trif, scarcely able to control her voice and not daring to lift her eyes from the work which she had resumed. "Whatever you like to talk about, you know I like to hear about. Aren't you my only sister, and my———"

"I didn't suppose that I talked much about Harry Trewman," said Fenie, making a pretense of sewing industriously.

"You mean nothing but what is entirely right, dear girl."

"Then why do you object to that innocent child hearing what I say? I'm sure that I say nothing which any one might not listen to—do I?"

"Certainly not; still, don't you remember what happened a night or two ago, dear, through a certain child hearing something and repeating it?"

"Yes, but—" here Fenie looked cautiously toward Trixy, who was reading, with an air of utter absorption—"but I'm not likely to speak so foolishly again. Trif, do let me take the cotton from that child's ears. It is making her uncomfortable. See. She is rubbing one of her ears now."

"She is sensible enough to complain when it really hurts. You don't imagine that her mother will let her suffer, do you?"

"No, but—well as I was saying, I don't really talk much about Harry Trewman, do I?"

Trif looked up so intently and roguishly that Fenie blushed deeply, and the blush remained while Trif said softly:

"Really, dear, you don't talk much about anything else."

"I don't see how you can say that," replied Fenie with uncertain voice, "when you know that I don't care anything—or not much, for him or about him. I don't suppose I would have spoken his name a single time this week if he hadn't come here last week, and if Trixy hadn't made that dreadful blunder. You certainly don't think me in love with him, I hope?"

"I hope not, dear. There are many gradations of feeling that a true woman must go through before she can say honestly that she is in love. But you—well, you like him a little better than you like any other of your admirers, don't you?"

"Ye—es, I suppose I do," replied Fenie, her voice not entirely under control. "He is gentlemanly, and honest-looking, and never brings the odor of liquor or tobacco with him. He doesn't make silly attempts at flattery, and he talks a great deal about his sisters, who are very nice girls, and he knows when to go home, instead of dawdling here until midnight, and we like the same books and pictures, so——"

"And so he is a pleasant acquaintance to have—too pleasant to lose entirely?"

"Yes, indeed, and if it hadn't been for that dreadful child—there, Trif, she's rubbing that ear again. I'm sure she's in pain. Do let me remove that ridiculous cotton."

"Tut, tut. Go on. You were saying——"

"Oh, what was I saying? What were we talking about?" asked Fenie, with charming but entirely transparent hypocrisy. "Oh, I was merely going to say that if Trixy hadn't made that dreadful speech to him the other night, I wouldn't have missed one delightful party—perhaps two, to which he and his oldest sister would have taken me."

"Oh, I see. 'Tis only the parties that trouble you."

"Tryphosa," exclaimed Fenie indignantly, as she arose from her chair, "I think you're real unkind—real tormenting. First you make fun of me for talking a lot about him, and then you make me talk about him a great deal more. I wasn't going to say a word about him this afternoon, but you've kept me at it in spite of myself. Perhaps you don't want me to like him. Well, I shan't oblige you. I do like him. I'm not a bit in love with him, but I do like him ever so much, and I'm not a bit ashamed to say so. There!"

"Bravo!" exclaimed Trif, springing from her chair and throwing her arms about her sister. "I'm glad that at last you know your own mind. Now stop acting like a child, and be the woman you have the right to be. I'm proud of you, my darling sister—proud of your honesty and spirit. But—why, my dear girl, what is the matter?"

"Harry's been driven away from here," sobbed Fenie, "and I'm dreadful unhappy about it, and I want him to come back."

"Hurrah," sounded a high childish treble. The sisters looked in the direction of the sound, and there stood Trixy, with glowing cheeks and dancing eyes as she continued:

"I want him to come back, too, for he promised to bring me a doll."

"Trixy," exclaimed Fenie severely. Trixy understood at once and looked guilty, but she explained:

"One of the cottons dropped out, and I didn't know a thing about it till you boo-hoo'd."

---

# CHAPTER III.
## UNAPPRECIATED.

"PHIL," said Trif from her pillow one morning very early, "are you awake?"

Phil half wished he wasn't, for he was just sinking into the morning's final doze, but loyalty compelled him to admit that he was not asleep.

"I'm so glad," responded Trif, "for I've thought out a plan for making matters right once more between Fenie and Harry."

"So have I, my dear, so between us we'll be sure to succeed. Now let's drop asleep again; if we talk much we'll get Trixy awake far too long before breakfast, which won't be good for her."

"There's no danger. The dear little thing sleeps soundly nowadays. What is your plan?"

"'Tis simply to invite him and his sister Kate to dinner."

"How stupid! You don't suppose he'll come after what he heard the last time he was here?"

"Won't come? Why not?"

"Because he was rudely driven away."

"Nonsense! Did you ever drive flies from sugar or sweetmeats? Didn't they return as soon as they saw a ghost of a chance?"

"I don't think the comparison is complimentary, either to my sister or to Harry."

"Why not? Fenie is the sweetest creature that I know of, except you, and if Harry can or will keep away from her he's not half the man I take him to be."

"But he certainly has some self-respect?"

"Yes, far too much to be discouraged by a single rebuff. Do you suppose I'd have lost you through any such reason as you think is keeping him away at present? I suppose he may be feeling dismal, poor fellow, but at the same time he's learning how much he cares for Fenie, which isn't a bad sort of knowledge for a young man to have. As to Fenie——"

"Sh——h——! I didn't mean to tell you about her, for the secret is hers, not mine, and——"

"But you couldn't keep anything from your husband, oh? Well, this heart is a safe place to come to with confidences."

"Phil, dear. Do be serious a moment!"

"I never was more serious in my life, my dear. Haven't I just ruined the last nap to which I was entitled? As to the young people, we'll have Harry and his sister to dinner as soon as you like. The sister will come, because she likes your dinners, your sister and you; Harry will come rather than explain to his sister. He and Fenie will feel so uncomfortable at first that they will be unusually affable to each other, and within half an hour they will be far better friends than ever before. Don't you see?"

"Upon my word," exclaimed Trif, with an impulsive kiss, "you're a born match-maker."

"Pshaw," exclaimed Phil, pretending not to be delighted with the compliment, "I'm merely a common-sense judge of human nature. If you'll only keep your irrepressible baby from hearing things in the meantime, and saying them to the wrong people, everything will go well."

"I'm sure I can't imagine how she can make any trouble. I'm sure that Fenie has given her cautions enough during the last week, to make the child afraid to say a word about anything to anyone who shouldn't hear it. At least once an hour, all day long, it has been 'Trixy, don't'—and 'Trixy, don't'—and——"

"Don't what, mamma?" drawled a gentle voice from a crib near the bed.

"Nothing, dear. Go to sleep again." The remaining conversation between husband and wife was conducted in soft whispers.

Several hours later Harry Trewman's sister Kate dropped in, "just for a moment." Kate was a wide-awake young woman, several years Fenie's senior. She had seen that something was troubling her brother, and it took very little time for her to determine that Fenie was the something. In Kate's opinion Harry, although little more than a year younger than she, was a mere boy who needed sisterly management, and Kate was not the woman to shirk any family duty.

Trif and Fenie chanced to be out shopping, and Kate was departing when Trixy came through the hall with some doll's garments which had just been laundered. Each looked at the other inquiringly, and Trixy said:

"Did you bring it?"

"Bring what, Trixy?"

"Why, the doll your brother Harry promised me. I thought maybe he sent it by you, seeing he doesn't come here any more."

"Doesn't come here any more?"

"No. Didn't he tell you?"

Kate hesitated a moment before answering. To extract information from a child or a servant seemed to her a very mean act—when other women did it. On the other hand, she owed loyal service to her brother, who was utterly incapable of managing his own affairs, so far as young women were concerned. Besides, Kate was sure that she was simply dying of curiosity, so she choked her sense of propriety and replied:

"I don't know until you make me fully understand what you are talking about."

"Why," said Trixy, opening her eyes very wide, "he learned a lesson here, and I taught it to him, though Aunt Fee said his sisters ought to have done it. 'Twas that young men oughtn't to go calling stormy evenings when young ladies don't expect company and put on their nicest dresses. He was going to give me a doll for teachin' him the lesson, but he hasn't sent it yet, and I've been hopin' for it ev'ry day, and thinkin' he'd bring it, but Aunt Fee says he won't come here any more, and she cried a whole lot about it the other day, and——. Why, don't you know it ain't polite to go away while somebody's talking to you? I'm 'stonished."

Kate had moved abruptly toward the door; she had learned all she wanted to know, and she was feeling very uncomfortable with the information which followed, so she said:

"Excuse me, Trixy, but I'm afraid you're telling me more than you should. Little girls shouldn't repeat all they hear; haven't your parents ever told you so?"

"Oh, yes," assented Trixy cheerfully; "they was dreadfully worried for fear I'd say something to the wrong people. The idea of it!" Trixy found the idea so funny that she laughed heartily; Kate at the same time wished she had not entered the house. She thought rapidly and said:

"Trixy dear, let's have a nice little secret between you and me. Don't say anything to anyone about our chat this morning, or that I've been here, until I say you may, and I will give you two dolls—half a dozen dolls, if you like, and then we'll both together tell the whole story to your mama and your Aunt Fenie, and have a great joke about it."

"Oh, good, good, good!" exclaimed Trixy, trying to climb up to Kate's face to kiss it, for Trixy was a grateful little thing, and dearly loved a joke and a secret, probably because she couldn't possibly keep either of them. She bestowed her kiss, with several others to keep it company, and Miss Trewman left the house just in time to meet Trif and Fenie about a hundred steps away. She passed them briskly, although with a cheery "Good morning," but in a moment she asked herself:

"I wonder if they'll suspect? Thank goodness, I didn't leave my card."


"Oh, Trif!" said Fenie. "She looked as if she had been at our house. I do hope she didn't meet Trixy."

"Fenie!" exclaimed Trif indignantly, although she had been impressed by the same hope, or fear, "don't act like an insane person. The entire world doesn't revolve about you and Harry Trewman."

Fenie was suppressed for the moment, but when she entered the house and saw Trixy capering ecstatically through the parlor, and singing shrilly:

Half a dozen dolls; Half a dozen dolls; Half a dozen, Half a dozen, Half a dozen dolls.

she exclaimed:

"Trixy, has any one been here?"

"I can't tell you, 'cause it's a secret. Say, Aunt Fee, ain't the Trewmans awful rich? I should think they must be, if one of them can give away six dolls at a time."

"Oh, Trif!" exclaimed Fenie, posing like a tragedy queen, "'twas just as I feared."

"Trixy," said Trif gently as she seated herself and drew the child to her side, "when Miss Trewman was here, did———"

"Why, has she let out the secret already? Dear me! Some grown folks are leaky, as well as little girls, aren't they?"

"She told me nothing," replied Trif, "so I want you to tell me what you said to her."


"But, mamma dear, I can't, 'cause it's a secret and both of us are to tell it to you together."

"When?" asked Fenie in a tone that made the child tremble as she replied:

"I don't know, but I hope awful soon, 'cause then she's goin' to give me—oh, I almost told."

"Almost told what?" Fenie demanded. "Don't you know that little girls have no right to keep things secret from their mothers?"

Trixy looked up pitifully. Fenie's face, which as long as Trixy could remember, had been full of smiles and dimples, was now stern and commanding. Trixy's eyes filled with tears, but Fenie's face remained stern and unrelenting.

"You don't want me to tell lies, I hope, and be burned a whole lot after I die?" sobbed the child.

"I'd almost rather you'd tell lies than repeat some things which you think are true."

"Fenie!" exclaimed Trif. Then it was Fenie's turn to cry. Trif banished her with a look, and then began to question the child; but just outside the door stood a young woman with the air of a person determined to hear whatever was said, no matter how true might be the old saying that listeners never hear any good of themselves.

"You may keep your secret, dear, or what is left of it," said Trif, taking Trixy upon her knee. "Mamma knows that Miss Trewman was here, but you did not tell her, so don't feel bad about it. I hope, though, that you didn't forget all that's been said to you about talking about family affairs to persons whom they don't concern."

"Why, mamma dear, I wouldn't do such a dreadful thing. But Miss Trewman's brother wasn't a thing that didn't concern her, was he?"

Fenie, outside the door, wiped her eyes and wrung her hands as Trif replied:

"That depends upon what you said about him."

"Why, I only said he didn't come here no more, and I was awful sorry, 'cause he promised me a doll, and I've been waitin' for it awful hard. And it wasn't wrong, was it, to say that Aunt Fee was awful sorry too, and cried a whole lot about it? You know the Trewman girls like Aunt Fee, ever so much."

There was a pronounced rustle in the hall, and Trif and Trixy hurried out just in time to see a sobbing girl hurrying up the stair. They followed her, but Fenie dashed into her own room, slammed the door, and shot the bolt with much unnecessary noise. She paid no attention to many knocks and gentle calls by her sister, so finally Trif sat down upon the top stair, placed her elbows on her knees and her face in her hands, and looked so unhappy that

Trixy cuddled to her side and kissed and caressed her. The child got no response, but a sad look which was so reproachful and prolonged that Trixy herself burst into tears and exclaimed:

"Oh, dear! I wish I hadn't ever come down from heaven, or done anythin', or anythin', or anythin'."

---

# CHAPTER IV.
## IN CHARGE OF EACH OTHER.

HARRY TREWMAN and his sister were invited to dine with the Highwoods, although Fenie declared that after what had been said to them, neither of them would think for an instant of coming. For herself, she was sure that she couldn't and wouldn't face them for all the world, and that she never wanted to see either of them again. Should they accept the invitation, Fenie declared that she would excuse herself with the sick headache, which she certainly would have on the occasion.

When, however, the Trewmans did decline, on the plea of a previous engagement, Fenie was so inconsistent as to declare that she was the most miserable person alive, and that she wished she was dead.

Then every one in the house, from the master down to the single servant, became wretched, for Fenie had always been a cheerful creature, romping with Trixy as if she herself was not more than seven years old, singing merrily throughout the day, and working harder than any hireling when there was work to be done.

Trif talked sensibly to the girl; Phil joked with her, but Trixy remained almost as silent as a mute, and looked as if she were laboring under a heavy load of remorse and contrition. Even her father's boisterous play, of which she was as fond as if she were a boy, was treated as if it was far too good for her, and as if she had no right to enjoy it. Then Phil began to worry.

"Trif," said he, "you must reason that child out of her remorse, or you'll have an invalid on your hands."

"I hope and pray that I may not, for I already have one invalid. I'm seriously frightened about Fenie. The only fault I've ever had to find with her was that she never would take things seriously, no matter how important they were, but now—oh, it seems as if all the seriousness of the Wardlow blood was concentrated in her, and all on account of the innocent blundering of that darling child. I know the affair is shattering her health, and sometimes I fear it is injuring her reason."

"Nonsense! Give her a change of some kind, and she'll recover quickly. At present she doesn't love that fellow, although I suppose she thinks she does—girls as young as she are very likely to mistake mere interest in a man for something more serious. Take her, and Trixy, on a little trip somewhere—run down to Florida and back. This is just the season for such a trip."

"Philip Highwood! You talk as if we were made of money. We haven't a fortune."

"But we have, my dear; we have two fortunes. Fenie is one and Trixy is the other, and I don't intend to lose either, if I can help it."

"A trip to Florida may cost all we've saved."

"What does that matter, if it saves Fenie and Trixy for us? "

Phil had his way in the end, for the good and sufficient reason that he and Trif loved each other so well that it took but a few moments' talk to make the way of one the way of both, no matter who devised it. The Florida trip cost Phil some pangs, for he had intended to start a country home in the spring—a modest one, but everything costs money in this practical world of ours. He did not look forward with pleasure, either, to being separated from his wife and child for a fortnight or more, for they had seldom been apart more than a single day; nevertheless, he kept all these things to himself, although he did much thinking about them.

As to the travelers, Trif assured Fenie, in entire honesty, that Phil was dreadfully troubled about Trixy's health, upon which Fenie made haste to show that she really could think of more than one thing at a time.

Trixy was informed, with equal care, but far more detail, that her Aunt Fee was quite ill, but that not a word was to be said about it in any circumstances, even to Aunt Fee herself.

"I know all about it," said the child, her eyes filling with tears, "and I was the dreadful little girl that made her sick. I thought lots about it, and prayed lots about it, and cried whole pillows-ful about it, but it hasn't done any good."

"Now is the time to do a lot of good, dear; you can mend your ways by trying to help mend Aunt Fee."

So it was arranged that Trixy should regard herself as her Aunt Fee's one special nurse during the Southern trip, and that Trif should be physician, to be consulted whenever necessary, although the best medicine, for the invalid, Trif declared, would be some of Trixy's chat and play.

"The best medicine she could have would be a long look at Harry Trewman's face," added Phil, as the child left the room. "If she———"

"I just came back, mamma," said Trixy, returning suddenly, "to tell papa that if Miss Trewman brings around them—I mean those—half a dozen dolls, that he'll express 'em to me, won't he? 'Cause I've told all my other dolls about it, and they look disappointeder and disappointeder every mornin' when they wake up. And papa'll send me any letters that come for me, won't he?" Then Trixy danced away again, while her father remarked:

"If that child's imagination keeps in growth with her body, there'll be a woman novelist in the family in the course of time."

Trif and Trixy and Fenie started for Florida by easy stages, Phil having told his wife that two or three stops could be made at places where a sorrowful girl of temperament naturally lively might have her thoughts diverted in spite of any determination to the contrary.

The first stop was at Old Point Comfort, which most young women who have been there prefer to call Fortress Monroe, for the largest fort in the United States is there, and within it are always thirty or forty officers, who, whether young or old, make delightful company of themselves, during their brief moments off duty, for all charming women at the enormous hotel which, with the fort, contains almost the entire population of Old Point Comfort. For the rest, there is little there but water and air—but such water and air! At one side of the fort is the James River, several miles wide, at the other side is Chesapeake Bay, so wide that one cannot see the other shore, while in front Hampton Roads extends ten miles away, to the outskirts of the ancient and picturesque city of Norfolk.

Fenie conscientiously intended to be unhappy, no matter where she might be, no matter how much attention she might give to Trixy. Besides, the party arrived at the Point about sunrise in early April, when scarcely any one was stirring, and the outside of a great hotel is not an inspiriting object to contemplate when there is no human being visible to relieve it.

Trixy, however, had not determined to be anything dreadful, so she was no sooner ashore and feeling the gentle sea breeze upon her cheeks and in her lungs, than she began running to and fro on the beach in front of the hotel, and tossing pebbles at Fenie, and even dropping a small pebble between Fenie's collar and neck, and Fenie called her a dreadful little wretch and began to chase her, for there was no one by to see, except Trif, who made no objection. The sea air had been stimulating Fenie, too, and before she had thought it possible to do anything inconsistent with sentimental dismalness she had acquired rosy cheeks, bright eyes, and an earnest longing for breakfast. As for Trif, she sought the telegraph office to wire her husband:

"Both invalids already much better."

After breakfast Trif chanced to meet an old acquaintance on the piazza. Fenie, by a violent effort, regained her sadness and declined to meet any one. As Phil had said that ladies and children could safely go about unattended at Old Point, Trif begged Trixy to take her Aunt Fee a long walk on the beach, and to play as freely as she liked. Then Trif begged Fenie to keep dear Trixy out of doors, under the mild sun and in the invigorating air, and Fenie was glad of an excuse to get away from other people, so the couple strolled along the beach, in the direction of the lighthouse and the water battery, enjoying the strangeness of everything they saw.

"What's that bird-cage on top of that funny little straight up-and-down house for?" asked Trixy, pointing to the lighthouse.

"That's not a bird-cage, dear. That is the light that the Government puts in its window here, to show the sailors the way home. It burns very brightly, and all night long."

"Dear me! What a big gas bill the Government must have to pay! Say, Aunt Fee, what's that big black thing on the grass, on the top of the wall of the fort?"

"That's a cannon."

"What is it for?"

"Oh, to kill bad people with."

"Gracious! Is there such lots of bad people down here as that? Papa said the place was so nice and safe."

"It is safe enough, dear, for us. The bad people that are shot with cannons come here from other countries."

"When do they come?"

"Oh, don't ask me," said Fenie, who was trying to keep from not keeping miserable, but was not succeeding very well.

"Who shall I ask?"

"Oh, one of the soldiers, I suppose."

Fenie sat upon a rock which formed part of a little breakwater, looked out to sea, and took a pensive attitude, while Trixy stood and stared at the cannon, and wondered, and wished she knew more about the killing of bad people by artillery.

Just then Lieutenant Bruce Jermyn, of the artillery service, came from the flank of the water battery and walked toward the hotel. He was no pink-faced, slender youth, like lieutenants in most military novels, but a handsome, stout, manly-looking fellow of about thirty-five years, like hundreds of other lieutenants of our army in time of peace. Trixy saw him, hurried to him, and said:

"Mr. Soldier, will you please tell me when you're going to kill some bad people with the cannon?"

"Eh?" said Jermyn, taking his cigar from his lips and raising his cap. "Oh, not until they come here and insist upon being killed, I suppose."

"Why? Do they insist upon bein' killed, and come here to have you do it for them?"

"Um—er—well, we like to be ready, in case they should come, although we hope they'll stay away. I beg your pardon, but will you tell me your name? You look very like some one whom I used to know."

"My name's Trixy Highwood, and that's Aunt Fee, sittin' on the rocks there, and——"

"And her last name is?——"

"Wardlow."

"Well, well." The officer did not sigh, but he looked reminiscent; then he took both of Trixy's hands, looked intently into the child's face, and said:

"I knew your mother about ten years ago."

"Oh, Aunt Fee." shouted Trixy. "Come here—quick! Here's one of mamma's friends."

The awakening was somewhat rude, but when Fenie turned her head and saw an officer approaching, with Trixy, she at once became a curious yet dignified young woman. She arose and met the couple, as Jermyn saluted and said:

"The child is to blame for this interruption, Miss Wardlow. I recognized her by her resemblance to her mother, whom I hope you may have heard speak of me. My name is Jermyn. My battery was stationed in New York Harbor a few years ago."

"Indeed!" exclaimed Fenie, in pleased surprise. She had heard frequently of the young officer whom Trif had admired greatly, before Phil Highwood had laid siege to her heart. Phil, too, had heard much about him, and feared him, as any civilian suitor fears a rival who wears a military uniform. Fenie had often wished she might one day meet the man of whom she had heard so much, and now she was face to face with him, and—really, what a fine-looking fellow he was!

"What's inside of them—the cannons?" asked Trixy.

"Nothing more dangerous than air," the officer replied.

"Children are so idiotically curious," said Fenie.

"Oh, merely naturally so. Mayn't I show your niece one of the guns?—and won't you accompany us? 'Tis but a step or two to the water battery. By the way, I hope that Mr. and Mrs. Highwood are here?"

"My sister is," Fenie replied. "We came down here hastily—indeed, we are on our way to Florida, for their dear child's health."

"I must do myself the honor of calling at once."

"Won't you wait," said Trixy appealingly, "until you show me the bad-people-killers?"

"Surely," replied Jermyn, "if afterward you will guide me to your mother."

The visit to the guns was prolonged to include a tour of the fort, about which Fenie was wildly curious, for she had never been inside of a fort, as her sister had in the days to which Jermyn had alluded, and she and Trif were such inseparable companions that she wished to know of everything that Trif knew. Jermyn proved to be capital company; besides, was he not a one-time admirer of Fenie's sister? Fenie felt entirely at ease with him, and she was delighted with the strangeness of everything she saw, so soon she was chatting as freely and cheerily as if she had never known a trouble.

Later in the morning Trif, seated on the piazza near the beach, was astonished to see her sister approaching with an army officer, with whom she seemed to be well acquainted. Soldiers looked very much alike to Trif; besides, she was so delighted at the sudden improvement in Fenie's appearance that she did not recognize Jermyn until her sister, with a roguish look, said:

"Trif, I'm astonished! Should auld acquaintance be forgot?"

"Mrs. Highwood!"

"Oh, Mr. Jermyn!"

Neither blushed, although Fenie had hoped they would. As for Trixy, who had not had much opportunity to talk during the walk through the fort, she looked intently at her invalid charge, her dear Aunt Fee. The instant there was a lull in the conversation, Trixy could not help saying:

"Mamma, seems to me that somethin's made Aunt Fee look awful weller all at once; don't you think so?"

Then the blushes, for which Fenie had looked in her sister's cheeks, hurried into her own, and refused to depart.

# CHAPTER V.
## A SURPRISE.

"HERE'S a letter for you, Harry," said Kate Trewman one morning as her brother came to the breakfast table, "and from the penmanship of the address I should imagine it to be from a washerwoman or a newsboy."

Harry looked solemnly at the address—he had looked solemnly at everything for several days, but when he saw the signature he started, a motion which did not escape the observant eye of his sister, who exclaimed:

"Do tell me what has happened! You look like an actor in a play with a great letter-scene in it."

Harry did not reply, for he was trying to read the letter, the writer of which could read, he knew, but seemed not to have learned to write, or even to spell, for the letter ran as follows:

"Dere Mister Trumen: I wunt to git yure pikcher an if yu giv it tu me yu needunt giv me that dolle tho I want the dolle lots an them yure sistur wus goin to gimme. Plese send me the pikcher rite away cause I'm goin a travelen. Youres trule

TRIXY HIGHWOOD."

"Do tell me what it is!" exclaimed Kate.

"'Tis a dead secret—or a mystery," Harry replied, with an absent-minded manner and a far-away look. Then he re-read the letter and laughed, at which Kate said:

"Thank goodness! Evidently it isn't a tragedy!"

"No, although there may be some elements of a drama in it."

"Do let me see the letter."

"Not now, dear girl. It is on a matter which I think should be regarded as strictly confidential."

Nevertheless Kate saw the letter before the day was done, and she did a lot of thinking about it. Then she drew her brother into the parlor and said abruptly:

"I've thought it all out. Fenie Wardlow hasn't a picture of you, has she?"

"Kate!" exclaimed Harry severely. "Do you imagine me to be conceited enough to present my portrait to young women in general?"

"Tut, tut! You know very well that Fenie Wardlow isn't classed in your mind among young women in general. She's the one and particular woman of all the world, to you. Answer my question; has she your picture?"

"No. Now are you satisfied?"

"Not entirely. Still, I'm sure she wants it. That child never wrote you of her own accord, to ask for your picture."

"Kate! Will you kindly remember that Miss Wardlow is a lady? I'm surprised that you should make such an insinuation."

"I've insinuated nothing, but there is something behind Trixy's letter. She's a very longheaded child, and the family adores her, and she is always with Trif and Fenie, and hears everything they say, so——"

"Do you really think that Miss Wardlow herself wanted a picture of me?" interrupted Harry.

"That is exactly what I do think. Oh, Harry! I didn't suppose a man could blush so splendidly! There, there—don't be ashamed of it; 'tis wonderfully becoming, and——"

Kate was an affectionate sister, so she stopped long enough to throw her arms about her brother and kiss him soundly. Then she continued:

"Send a picture to the child at once—and do send that doll also. I'd send with it the lot that I promised, if I wasn't afraid that the family would ask questions, and I would be dreadfully mortified if they were to learn that I questioned Trixy closely on a certain subject several days ago. I wish I knew what the child means by saying that she's going travelling. I wonder if—oh, well, I'll make some calls elsewhere, and find out all about it."

Meanwhile Trif, Trixy and Fenie were postponing their further journeying southward. Old Point Comfort is a hard place to leave; one finds old friends, learns that new ones are coming; so the days slip by delightfully. The air seemed to be doing wonders for both Fenie and Trixy, and Trif was enjoying herself as a clever young woman always can where good company abounds, and she can give her entire time to it. Besides, Lieutenant Jermyn assured her that the season was so far advanced that she would find Florida uncomfortably hot.

Jermyn had also put Trif entirely at ease by not showing a bit of sentimentality over the woman he had loved and lost. He was so entirely himself in her presence that she imagined him happily married, although she did not like to question him on the subject. He was quite attentive to Fenie, too, and made haste to introduce several brother officers, who made themselves interesting, so Fenie seldom was without the attendance of some man in uniform. Her admirers were not all young, either, for admiration of womanhood appears to be one of the original elements of the military nature, so several elderly officers frequently sought the society of Fenie and her sister, and as Fenie was the younger, and unmarried, she innocently took all the admiration to herself. Finally, when a retired admiral, himself as young at heart and engaging in conversation as any of his juniors, paid special attention to Fenie, that young woman became so exuberant of cheerfulness that she read herself a severe lecture, almost at midnight, when there was no one else for her to talk to.

How dreadfully she was neglecting Trixy, too! She had promised to watch the child carefully, yet Trixy ran at will upon the beach, and buried herself in sand, and several times a day she ventured close enough to the water to wet her feet, and Fenie was always going to keep her from doing so again, but Trif was the only one who did it. Fenie told herself that she was becoming a dreadfully selfish girl, but really she never seemed to find time to do anything that ought to be done.

Trixy did such dreadful things, too. She had learned the names of all the colored men who brought sail-boats to the hotel pier when the water was smooth and the breeze gentle. She seemed fascinated by the picturesque raggedness of the few colored people who lounged in the single street of the little village. She had no hesitation about introducing herself to any one who spoke to Trif or Fenie, she talked almost as much as if she were at home; and what mightn't she say if the impulse came to her? Trif was begged to caution the child, that there was nothing to tell; then to make assurance doubly sure, Fenie herself cautioned her.

"I don't tell nobody nothin', Aunt Fee," protested Trixy. "Really and truly, I don't. I only told Lieutenant Jermyn and a lot of them that you was awful sick, and that was why we came down here."

"I sick? You dreadful child! Don't you know that it was on account of your own bad health that we came?"

"Oh, Aunt Fee! You're awful mistaken—indeed you are. You must have got us mixed up some way, 'cause papa and mamma said 'twas you that was sick. I just came along to take care of you, and I've been doin' it with all my might."

"Indeed! And what was the matter with me, I wonder?"

"Why—y—y!" exclaimed the child, opening her eyes very wide. "Do you forget things as easy as that? Mamma said you'd go crazy if you didn't stop thinkin' about Harry Trewman, and papa said the best medicine for you would be a trip off to somewhere—the best, except one thing."

"Except what thing?"

"Oh, nothin'."

"Don't say that. Tell me the truth at once."

"I can't, else I'll spoil a s'prise."

"What surprise?"

"I mustn't tell, else there won't be no s'prise."

"Oh, Trixy! Surprises are such stupid things! People usually find out all about them before they occur."

"Nobody'll find out this one, I guess, unless Harry—say, Aunt Fee, whereabouts is the post-office here?"

"All letters come to the hotel. What were you going to say about Harry? Harry who?"

"Why, don't you know? Then I can't tell, 'cause that's part of the s'prise."

"Trixy, tell me this instant!"

Trixy looked troubled for a moment; then she dashed out of the room, and Fenie, who had been dressing while she talked, could not follow. Trixy found her mother, who handed her a letter of such size that the retired Admiral, who was chatting with Trif, remarked:

"How large a letter for so small a lady to receive. I hope, Miss Trixy, that you haven't a love affair on your mind?"

"No, indeed, sir. Other folk's love affairs are enough for me to attend to." Then the child slipped away, while Trif continued to wonder from whom had come the letter which Phil had forwarded, and which appeared to contain a large photograph.

Trixy retired to the hotel, opened her letter, and found, as she had expected, a picture of Harry Trewman. There was some writing on the back of the card, and Trixy wished she knew what it was, but all chirography was as undecipherable to her as Hebrew; her own letters were written in imitation of print. She roamed about the corridors in search of some acquaintance whose education was broader than her own, and finally she chanced upon Lieutenant Jermyn, who had been visiting an invalid friend.

"Say, Mr. Jermyn, you can read writin', can't you?"

"Sometimes, Trixy, sometimes."

"Then won't you tell me what's on the back of this picture?"

Jermyn read aloud: "My dear little girl, I am very fond of you, and I shall be glad to have you carry my picture on your journey with you, so that I may be brought to your mind once in awhile. Yours sincerely, HARRY TREWMAN."

"Oh, I'm so glad he sent it!" exclaimed Trixy. Jermyn smiled and replied:

"Upon my word, Miss Trixy, you're beginning quite early to be interested in young men."

"You're the second person who's made that mistake," Trixy replied. "The picture isn't for me; it's for Aunt Fee."

"Indeed!" Jermyn looked grave a moment or two before he continued, "Wouldn't it be better, then, for you not to show it to people in general?"

"Oh, I'm not going to. I only wanted to know what the writin' was about."

"Suppose you put it into the envelope," suggested Jermyn, "and take it to your aunt's room."

"Just what I was goin' to do," said Trixy. "Isn't it funny that both of us thought of the same thing?"

Jermyn admitted that it was, although he was oppressively silent as he walked through the hall—he who had always told Trixy some funny story when he met her.

Fenie had learned to like Jermyn greatly during their short acquaintance, but on the evening that followed the picture incident he surpassed himself in deference, humor and brilliancy. Fenie did not wonder that Trif had always remembered him pleasantly. She did wish he was not quite so old; a man of thirty-five seems dreadfully ancient to a girl of twenty. Still, soldiers were splendid anyway. Of course, he did not care particularly for her, for he had never seen her until that week, but there was something in his voice and manner on this particular evening that affected her strangely. Could it be that he was falling in love with her? If so, she—she really ought to feel sorry.

But was she? She could scarcely believe so; she would examine her mind seriously when the evening ended; perhaps she would speak to Trif about it. There was nothing between her and Harry Trewman—she could honestly say that, and perhaps—perhaps she had acted very foolishly about that young man. Harry was a fine fellow, as young men go, but how plain he appeared, to her mind's eye, beside the handsome soldier who scarcely left her side that evening!

By the time the evening ended the young woman had a head full of pleasing fancies marred only by a weak compunction of conscience. She sat in Trif's room a few minutes, chatting with her sister about people whom they had met during the day, and admiring Trixy, who was always a charming picture when asleep. Then she passed into her own room; in a moment Trif heard a sharp exclamation, and Fenie stood in the doorway between the rooms, gasping:

"What is the meaning of this?"

"Of what? Oh, my sister, you're looking like a ghost!"

"I feel as if I had seen one. Why did you do it? What have I done to———"

"Tryphena Wardlow, what are you talking about?" asked Trif, approaching the girl. "Do say something intelligible, if you can, and stop acting."

For answer, Fenie took her sister's hand and led the way to the mirror, between the glass and frame of which was a photograph of Harry Trewman.

"In the name of all that's mysterious," exclaimed Trif, "where did it come from?"

"Where, indeed! Didn't you place it there, to—to———"

"I give you my word that I never saw it, or knew of its existence, until this instant."


"Oh, this is dreadful," exclaimed Fenie, sinking into a chair. "There's some mystery about it. Who can be here who knows anything about—about what had happened? Who has been able to get into our room without our knowledge? I shan't dare to fall asleep. I shan't———"

"Do stop being dramatic, Fee, and try to be sensible. The picture didn't sneak in through the keyhole, nor did invisible hands bring it, although I confess that for the moment I'm mystified. Oh, I have it! Mark my words, Trixy knows something about that picture."

In an instant Fenie was in the adjoining room and shaking Trixy. The child was sleeping as soundly as ocean air and the lullaby of gentle surf can make children sleep, but Fenie persevered.

"Picture?—in your lookin' glass?" the child drawled. "Oh, yes; I put it there. That was the s'prise—that I wouldn't—tell you all about. Did it s'prise you—lots?"

"Yes—yes. But how did you get it?"

Trixy was falling asleep again, and her mother insisted that further explanation should be deferred until morning. As Fenie took the picture from the mirror she saw the inscription and read it. Then Bruce Jermyn went out of her mind and a joyous feeling took his place.

# CHAPTER VI.
## ALL BY CHANCE.

"I'VE found out all about them," said Kate Trewman to her brother, a day or two after Trif, Trixy and Fenie had gone South. "They've gone to Florida, for Trixy's health."

"Who have gone to Florida?" asked Harry, trying to appear indifferent.

"Whom do you suppose I mean? Mrs. Highwood, and Trixy, and Fenie. That child is the apple of their eye. Still, I'm inclined to think that Fenie herself wanted to get away for a while. I'm sure if I'd been in her place I'd have wanted to, had I known that certain other people knew certain things."

"What people? What things?"

"Oh, don't be silly."

"Well, my dear, I've been thinking of going South myself—oh, no; not to Florida. Our firm have a little business at Norfolk that requires personal attention, and they want me to attend to it. Don't you want to go with me? Old Point Comfort is within an hour's sail of Norfolk, and our friends, the Braymans, went down there yesterday, to remain a week, and there's a big fort there, full of officers, who are said to work harder and enjoy their leisure better than any other men in the United States."

"We go," said Kate, and go they did, the very next day.

Meanwhile, in entire ignorance of what some of their acquaintances were doing, Trif and Fenie found some small shopping necessary; the nearest shopping centre to Old Point was Norfolk. So one morning to Norfolk they went, taking Trixy with them.

Grown people's shopping is very tiresome business to little people, so Trixy became so uncomfortable that she begged to be allowed to rest by standing upon the sidewalk and looking at the passers-by, and Trif permitted it, stipulating that the child should not go further from the store than the street at either side.

The child soon found herself having a delightful time, and storing her mental picture book with unfamiliar scenes, when suddenly she shouted, "Hooray!"

Then she dashed across the street, and with one hand pulled the frock of Kate Trewman, while with the other she grasped Harry's sleeve.

"Trixy Highwood! Did you drop down from the sky?"

"I s'pose I did," said Trixy, after a moment of thought, "but that was seven years ago. To-day, though, I dropped over here from Old Point Comfort."

"But how do you come to be roaming the streets of Norfolk?" asked Kate.

"I ain't roamin'. I can't go off of this block, 'cause mamma and Aunt Fee are in the store there, buyin' things."

"But we thought you'd gone to Florida?"

"Oh, we're goin' there one of these days, I s'pose, 'cause that's where we started for; but mamma says it's hard to get away from Old Point, because she keeps findin' old friends there."

"Does Fenie find any?" discreetly asked Kate.

"She doesn't need to," was the reply, "for she keeps findin' new ones all the time. Say, army officers is real nice; don't you think so?"

"So I've always heard," said Kate, while Harry looked so unhappy that his sister pinched him until he complained. Just then Trif came out of the shop, wondering whether Trixy did not need looking after; but she lost none of her self-possession when she found herself face to face with the Trewmans. Within five minutes Trif had made the Trewmans promise to run over to Old Point before they returned to New York. She begged them, also, to return with her to the shop, and surprise Fenie, but Harry pleaded extreme haste—a matter of business, he said.

"Still," said Kate, "we may yet surprise her if you won't allude to us until you meet us at Old Point."

"That will be splendid," exclaimed Trif, with glowing cheeks; for she was thinking over the scene with Harry's picture.

"Harry," said Kate, as soon as the party separated, "you've no reason to worry."

"No reason!" echoed the young man. "I think I've a lot of them. Don't you remember what Trixy said about army officers?"

"Oh, to be sure!" Then Kate lapsed into silence.

"Trixy, dear," said Trif, before re-entering the shop, "I want you now to be very, very womanly. You mustn't say a word to Aunt Fee about the people we've just met."

"I understand, mamma dear. Say, when's Mr. Trewman and Aunt Fee goin' to be married?"

"Sh—h—h! Perhaps never. Who put such an idea into your mind?"

"Why, Bridget did—our servant, at home; but I thought of it before, 'cause they act just like the folks in the stories that you and Aunt Fee read out loud to each other sometimes."

Trif looked despairing—almost desperate. Her cautions must be intensified, so she continued.

"Remember, dear! Don't say a word about the Trewmans to Aunt Fee when we return to the shop. Don't mention them on the boat on the way back. Don't mention them in the hotel. Don't——"

"Oh, mamma!" interrupted Trixy. "What an awful lot of dont's! I wish I didn't ever see anythin', or hear anythin', or know anythin'."

"Poor, dear little girl," said Trif caressingly. "Grown people sometimes have 'dont's,' and have a lot of trouble with them, too."

"Is that so?" the child asked. "Do you ever have to put cotton in your ears, or bite your tongue?"

"You afflicted darling," exclaimed Trif, her maternal instinct fully aroused. Was her precious darling to be physically afflicted through affairs in which she had no part?—suffer for other people's affairs, for which she was not in any way responsible? No, indeed. She would give Fenie a lecture, and at once, which would do that young woman much good and save an innocent little girl from further torment. Fenie should learn to hold her own tongue; it was she who did most of the talking which poor little Trixy was obliged to hear—how could the child help hearing it? Sisterly affection was quite right; Trif had long tried to be sister and mother too to her pretty, darling sister, but should a child suffer for an adult,—the weak for the strong? Not while the weak, the child, was Trif's own, only daughter. Trixy should have no more trouble about the affairs of other people.

Full of this determination, Trif returned to the shop with an air so resolute and aggressive that the clerks shrank in terror and wondered what complaint was about to be made. She strode like a pictured goddess to where Fenie was idly wondering which of two patterns of insertion to buy; she turned her sister toward her and exclaimed, softly yet tragically:

"Tryphena, I must ask you to keep your affairs to yourself hereafter, except at such times as you and I are alone together. This poor child mustn't be tormented with them any longer. She——"

"Yes," said Trixy, "I've got to bite my tongue a lot more now, 'cause I just saw—oh, mamma, please don't pinch me so hard!"

"What did you see, Trixy?" asked Fenie.

"That piece of insertion you have in your hand—" said Trif quickly. "Trixy, dear, go back to the door, if you like—that piece of insertion, as I was saying, is just what I would get if I were you, for—" and the remaining conversation was closely restricted to garments, although Fenie looked somewhat indignant and curious.

The evening chanced to be one of the most delightful that had ever blessed Old Point. The sky was clear, the air warm yet invigorating; the music was of the best, the guests were in the best of humor with one another, and everything went as merrily as the traditional marriage bell.

Best of all, to one small person. Trixy had received permission to remain with the older people until nine o'clock, for she had complained that the nine o'clock gun at the fort always woke her, and Trif thought it a shame that the dear child had to be roused from sleep in a strange place, where she was alone, and Fenie said she was quite willing to sit beside Trixy's bed until the dear child fell asleep, and Trif did not dare to admit that her one consuming desire was that Fenie and Trixy should not be alone together a single instant until——

So Trixy remained up and awake, and Trif had no more thought of it than if she had been an inhabitant of another planet and without any right or title to a little girl who sat or stood near her all the while, as mute as a mouse, and also as observant. Bless congenial company! What wonders has it not wrought for tired men and women? Trif had not imagined herself tired when she started for the South, but woman's work is never done while woman is at home. So when she finds herself so far from it that she cannot by any possibility attend to it, yet can drop it from her mind, how she does enjoy the chat of other good women similarly situated!

As to Fenie, she was the centre of a little group of officers from the fort. Her sister was with her, and, although to some of the party the older sister was the more interesting of the two, she who was the younger and unmarried, assumed all the admiration was as entirely for her as if there were no other women at Old Point. Those officers did say such clever and delightful things! As to that, so did two or three civilians who joined the party, but there was something about a uniform that—oh, Fenie couldn't explain it, but she was sure that any other girl in similar circumstances would understand exactly what she meant.

Besides, was there not in the edge of the mirror the photograph of a man to whom her heart was entirely loyal, although no allegiance had ever been demanded? Others might be men, but he—he was Harry Trewman, the only man she had ever—no, not the only man she had ever loved, for she could not truly say, as yet, that she really loved Harry.

Just as some one had told a very amusing story, and Fenie had laughed heartily at it, and begun to tell a story of which the first had reminded her, she stopped and turned pale. Her sister wondered what was the matter, and soon learned, for, through the parlor, on the way to one of the corridors, and preceded by a porter with bags and wraps, came Harry Trewman and Kate. Fenie moved from the circle—moved as if she were in a dream. She extended her hand to Harry, who took it gravely, respectfully, for a fraction of a second, and then hurried after his sable guide. Fenie dropped back to her chair, resumed the story she had been telling, and completed it with such a mass of detail that, when finally the party broke up, one of the junior officers told a comrade that Miss Wardlow had evidently met her fate, and met him that very evening, too.

It was Fenie who broke up the party, for she was sure Trixy ought to be in bed—was it not after ten o'clock? No, indeed; Trif should not take the child to the room; hadn't she herself promised to look carefully after the dear little invalid?

Nevertheless, Trif herself was in the room within a few minutes. She found Trixy in bed, and Fenie kneeling beside her, and Trixy was talking, and Trif did not like to interrupt, because sometimes Trixy said things so odd that her mother liked to hear without seeming to notice.

"Trixy, Trixy," Fenie had just said. "It is very late, and you must be very sleepy. Don't you think you can drop off now?"

"I—s'pose so," the child drawled, "but there was somethin' I wanted to ask you. Let me see; what was it? Oh!" and Trixy sprang up and suddenly became very wide awake. "Say, Aunt Fee, did lookin' at him make you well?"

"Looking at whom, Trixy? I'm not ill, child?"

"Why, papa said a look at Harry Trewman's face was the best medicine you could have."

Fenie burst into tears, upon which Trif hurried to her, but Fenie continued to weep, and for so long that Trif wept too, after which Trixy sobbed pitifully.

"Papa said it, and she's had the look, and it ain't done her no good, for she's cryin' like ev'rythin', and I worked so hard to give it to her, and gave up a dolly to get it, and then he came himself, and that made her cry more than ever."

"Oh, Trif," exclaimed Fenie. "He met me so coldly—and after what he wrote on his picture, too! Do you suppose he was jealous of the company he saw me in?"

"Did Harry write you somethin' on a picture, Aunt Fee?" asked Trixy.

"Yes, he——; but you mustn't ask questions about things that don't concern you, Trixy."

"Oh, I won't, but I just wanted to know———"

"But you mustn't want to know what———"

"But———"

"Sh—h—!" Don't ever mention the subject to me again. Promise me, this instant!"

"Sister," protested Trif, "you don't yet know how that picture came to you."

I don't want to know anything about the picture, or him, or about———"

"Then I shan't tell you, or ask you, or anythin'," said Trixy, with a sob that would have softened any heart but that of a young woman who thought she had been treated coldly by the man whom she thought she might learn to love.

# CHAPTER VII.
## MORE REVELATIONS.

WHEN Harry Trewman reached his room he dropped into a chair and a very dismal frame of mind, which his face reflected, for when his sister looked in upon him a few minutes later she said:

"Why, brother! What is the matter with you? From your melancholy appearance one would suppose you hadn't just reached Old Point and its chief attraction."

"Attraction, indeed," moaned Harry. "I suspect I am a fool, for it never before occurred to me that a young woman whom I think the sum total of everything good and charming, might appear equally attractive to other men. Did you see the crowd about her?—the uniforms and buttons?—and how she seemed to be enjoying herself? Still, she has the right to do entirely as she likes; I've no claim upon her."

"My dear Harry," said Kate tenderly, as she seated herself on the arm of Harry's easy chair, "don't be foolish. Do you suppose that a girl is going to lose interest in everything and everybody in the world because she likes a certain young man, or because a certain young man likes her?"

"No. But she seemed to be enjoying herself so hugely. I never saw her so radiant."

"But why shouldn't she have enjoyed herself? I'm sure that I'd have done the same had I been in her place. I envy her the chance of talking with a lot of clever men. Do you think I would refuse it even if I were deeply in love with some one?"

"No, I suppose not; but that would be different."

"How?"

"Oh, you're a very decided young woman, with opinions of your own, while——"

"Every woman should be as you say I am if she would have men respect her. But, Harry, what fine fellows those soldiers are! They look as if they had minds of their own, and if there's anything that a woman specially likes in a man, it is that."

"Umph! I suppose you mean that young men who aren't soldiers haven't minds of their own—eh?"

"Harry, I think your own mind needs additional strength at once, which it may get from sleep. Go to bed. Good night. Sleep well."

Kate herself remained awake a long time, thinking about her brother's prospects, for she had been half in love several times, and been rescued by the discovery that some other man who seemed to admire her was more interesting than the man she thought herself specially fond of. She loved her brother dearly, but Harry was still young and boyish—none too much so, to be sure, for Fenie Wardlow, but how much more interesting those officers were! Her knowledge of them had been obtained during the several minutes in which she had sat at one end of the great parlor while Harry had been registering their names at the office and arranging for rooms, but she was a young woman who reached conclusions rapidly.

Like most other people who lie awake late to think, Kate awoke early. She peeped through the window blinds, inhaled the fresh air, and wished herself out of doors. Dressing quickly she went upon the verandah. The sky was clear, the air balmy, and the surf rippling brilliantly and murmurously on the beach. Kate noted all this and keenly enjoyed it. Then she chanced to see, on the higher and drier sands, almost at her feet, a large straw hat under which was a small frock, two little hands and a shovel. The little figure's back was toward her, but the figure's voice was high in air, and it was singing:

Half a dozen dolls; Half a dozen dolls; Half a dozen, Half a dozen, Half a dozen dolls.

"'Tis Trixy Highwood!" exclaimed Kate to herself, and she hastily descended to the beach and Trixy.

"Oh, Miss Trewman," shouted Trixy when she saw Kate, "don't you like to dig wells? It's awful fun. I've got this one nearly deep enough for the water to come in; as soon as it's done I'll lend you my shovel and you can dig one. Whoever digs the best one any day gets a five-cent piece from the Admiral—he comes around and looks at 'em ev'ry day. I won't mind if yours is better than mine and gets the prize."

Kate had no intention to take part in competitive well-digging, but she was glad to do anything that would give her sufficient excuse to be with Trixy a little while; so as there was not another person in sight except one of the hotel watchmen, she stretched herself upon the warm, dry sand, took Trixy's shovel, and began to dig.

"I'm so glad you came down," said Trixy. "Ev'rybody here sleeps so late, that it's lonesome on the beach in the mornin'. The sunrise gun always wakes me, and when I dress, mamma lets me out of the room if I promise to go back and wake her at 8 o'clock. It's fun to run up and down on the beach, and dig wells, and find pretty stones."

"Is it always so quiet as this in the morning?" Kate asked.

"Yes, indeed; there's scarcely anybody here, even as late as mamma comes down. Lots of folks don't eat breakfast until noon-time; how do you s'pose they manage to wait? Say; why didn't you make your brother come down and dig a well? Mamma says he looks as if he needed exercise."

"H'm! Really I hadn't thought of it."

"He does need exercise, though, don't he? But of course he does, if mamma says so. Besides, he looks real white. All the men here look kinder red and brown, 'specially the officers."

"You seem very observant of men, little girl—and of officers."

"Of course I am, 'cause I like 'em. Mamma likes 'em, too, and so does Aunt Fee, I guess, 'cause they're all the time talkin' to her, and walkin' on the piazza and the beach with her."

"They? Then there are more than one?"

"Gracious, yes! There's about forty here, Lieutenant Jermyn says."

"Lieutenant Jermyn? Who is he?"

"He's the first one I met, and he used to know mamma very well, and he's ever so nice to me, and he don't seem to know how to keep away from Aunt Fee—so I heard a lady say."

"Indeed." Kate continued digging a moment or two longer, for she wanted to think. Besides, the warm sea air was working its witchery with her, and disinclining her to effort. The sand was clean, she and Trixy were still the only occupants of the beach, so Kate soon sank entirely upon the warm white couch which old Ocean had provided for those who chose to recline upon it.

The sun was bright and she was without veil or parasol, but she could trust her complexion to itself for a few moments. There were so few times and places for a young woman out of doors! How delightful it would be, she thought, if somewhere near New York there was a great, clean, safe beach to lounge upon! The mere act of breathing seemed a positive pleasure. The sunlight, through her closed eyelids, became a delightful immensity of rosy pink, the ripple of the wavelets upon the beach was ideal music, the——

"Hello!"

It was Trixy who spoke, from not three feet away, but Kate pretended not to hear; she preferred the companionship of her own thoughts, although everything definite had escaped from them. The next sound she heard caused her to rise hastily on one elbow, for it seemed that there was a noise in the sand unlike that made by Trixy's shovel.

"Hello, Mr. Jermyn. Don't you know Miss Trewman? She's one of mamma's and Aunt Fee's friends."

"Don't arise, please," said Jermyn with a bow while Kate looked uncomfortable. "I'm glad to see that Trixy isn't the only visitor who has learned which is the most delightful hour of the day down here."

Kate persisted in arising, and Jermyn made haste to bring her a chair; then he talked well-digging in a matter-of-fact way with Trixy, and smiled, with Kate, at some of the child's replies, and so succeeded quickly in dispelling Kate's sense of embarrassment. Still more, wasn't he the very officer Kate had most noticed during her several minutes' survey the night before?

"You ought to like him lots, Miss Trewman," said Trixy suddenly, with the air of having recalled something from the limbo of forgetfulness, "'cause he likes Aunt Fee lots."

"And Aunt Fee's sister, too," added Jermyn, without change of countenance. "I had the pleasure of meeting Mrs. Highwood frequently, some years ago, when my battery was stationed at New York."

"How pleasant," said Kate, although she did not mean it. Again she wondered whether there might not have been deep purpose in that Florida trip which seemed to have ended at Fort Monroe. Something ought to be done, and at once, if it were not already too late. What should it be? Thinking was not easy, under the circumstances, for Jermyn was talking to her—not persistently, or as a man who was trying to flirt; and she liked his looks so much that she did not want to appear inattentive, although, really, didn't it seem utterly dreadful to be chatting before seven in the morning with a man who had been introduced only by a little girl?

As they talked, Kate resolved upon a plan of action. Fenie should become her sister-in-law if she, Kate, could manage it. Dear Harry should not be disappointed; Fenie was too young to marry a man like Lieutenant Jermyn. If Jermyn's attention could by any possibility be diverted from Fenie, she, Kate, would divert it; the result might be a heartache for herself, for she did most heartily admire such men. Still, she would endure such a pain, for her

dear brother's sake, and if, after all, the affair didn't end in a heartache, why—
—

Just here she blushed, although Jermyn couldn't imagine why, for at that very instant he was explaining, at Kate's request, why the fort on the Rip-Raps, a couple of miles away, had not been completed, and he could not imagine what there was in the subject, or in his description, to bring a blush to any cheek, yet he said to himself that the blush was very becoming, and that Miss Trewman was quite an interesting young woman.

The chat continued until Trixy, who had once in ten minutes asked Jermyn the time, announced that she must go to wake her mother for breakfast. This reminded Kate that she had a brother to rouse, so she and the child went into the house.

Half an hour later, while Trif and Fenie and Trixy with Jermyn, whom they had invited to breakfast with them, were chatting over their morning meal the head waiter brought Harry and Kate to the same table. There was no help for it, although Harry looked as if he wished there were; a head waiter is autocrat of his domain. As to the others, Trif exclaimed:

"How delightful!" Fenie smiled pleasantly, although with some embarrassment, while Trixy shouted:

"Hooray!"

Kate bravely began operations at once. Fortune, in the guise of the waiter, had placed her beside Jermyn and Harry beside Fenie, so, Kate argued, if she were to monopolize the officer, Harry and Fenie would be obliged to talk to each other, and she was old enough to know that compulsory conversation has frequently broken the thickest of social ice.

The plan worked finely. Harry and Fenie were obliged to talk to each other, for no one else spoke to either, and as each was determined that the other shouldn't think anything unusual the matter, each quickly became voluble and merry. Bless the transparency of youthful hypocrisy. Neither of those two young people imagined that any one was noticing them, yet Kate's heart was dancing with joy as she saw them frankly exchange tender looks, and Trif's mind lost a great weight so rapidly that she felt several years younger within half an hour, and she was made still happier when, as the entire party strolled toward the fort to see "guard mount," Jermyn had occasion to whisper to her:

"Mr. Trewman is a remarkably fortunate young man—bless him."

Guard mounting in the army is quite as ceremonious a matter as parade, and Jermyn had to answer many questions which Kate put in rapid succession, while Fenie, who had seen guard mount several times, explained everything to Harry. Trixy seemed interested only in the movements of a dog, which persisted in following every movement of the post band. Her mother gazed at her in adoration. How entirely the dear child seemed absorbed in whatever interested her—how oblivious to everything else!

When the ceremony ended, and the little crowd under the live-oak trees broke up, Fenie and Harry, Kate and Jermyn, began to move slowly toward the hotel, while Trif and Trixy walked behind them. Suddenly, while no one else was talking, Trixy remarked:

"Mamma, dear; wouldn't it be nice if they all got married, and——"

"Sh—h—!"

Kate suddenly asked Jermyn why it was that so large a fort had only a single flag-staff, and Harry hastened to give Fenie the details of a lumber contract concerning which he had come South, and Fenie listened as intently as if she knew lumber from timber, or any other commodity.

# CHAPTER VIII.
## A SNATCH AT TIME'S FORELOCK.

BETWEEN the exhilarating effects of the breakfast-table chat with Fenie, and the furtive, embarrassed, yet roguish look which Fenie had worn for a fraction of a second, when Trixy had made her unexpected remark in the fort about marriage, Harry Trewman was the happiest youth in the State of Virginia.

Nevertheless, he did not forget his business duties or his business training. The lumber case at Norfolk had disturbed his dreams at night, and was now troubling his day-dreams; the best way to avoid any more annoyance was to hurry over to Norfolk and settle the business at once.

Besides, now seemed the proper time to come to a definite understanding with Fenie—an understanding of the kind frequently completed by the presentation of a ring containing a stone, preferably a diamond. Harry had seen in a Norfolk shop a ring, which he thought would entirely answer the purpose, and he would buy it that very morning. Before he started, however, he took the precaution to beg his sister, half shamefacedly, to keep all designing bachelors from Fenie for a few hours.

"Trust me for that," said Kate, in her most earnest manner. "I shall keep Fenie under my own wing to-day; I shall make sure, at least, that Lieutenant Jermyn doesn't injure any of your chances."

Kate was as good as her word, and as she and Fenie were really very fond of each other, they were together all morning. Trixy was with them; her honest little heart was still full of the injunction to take the best of care of her Aunt Fee, but the child found little to do but sit still and listen. The two young women talked as freely and incessantly as any other couple of old acquaintances, amid scenes entirely new, and with plenty of time at their disposal, and Trixy heard much that set her to thinking; but she had so often been cautioned against asking questions, since she had been at Old Point, that she found it necessary to think out her puzzles for herself.

Kate's principal cause of fear, also her principal object of admiration, Lieutenant Jermyn, did not reappear during the morning, and Kate was mystified, as well as somewhat troubled. Was it possible that he preferred to chat with Fenie only while her sister was present—or when he could find her alone? If so, matters were more serious than Kate had thought. Perhaps—but, pshaw!—Kate rebuked herself with an indignant blush, for the thought that perhaps Jermyn might desire to chat with Kate herself, and preferred not to talk to two young women at once.

Yet she continued to wonder. Like most other young women, and, indeed, like all Americans not well acquainted with the army, she was of the impression that officers had nothing to do, while not on parade, but make themselves pleasing to the general eye, and to young women in particular. She did not know that most of the officers at Fort Monroe were either instructors or students at a most exacting post-graduate school of artillery, where each was expected to impart or receive such advanced knowledge as would suffice the commandant of a great fort or the chief of artillery of an army.

As Kate wondered, and feared, and imagined it occurred to her that the most sensible course would be to "draw out" Fenie. She felt toward the girl as any young person feels toward one several years younger; she had a sense of condescension and tolerance which was not always under good control. Fenie was young, so she was artless, unsuspecting, and transparent. What would be easier than to learn from her, not for curiosity's sake, but for Harry's and Fenie's own, all that there might be between her and Lieutenant Jermyn?

So, as the two girls finally seated themselves on the piazza to look at the noonday promenaders, Kate asked suddenly:

"What becomes of all the men here in the middle of the day?"

"Oh, they are somewhere with one another, I suppose," replied Fenie. "Men are very interesting to one another, don't you think so? There's a club in the fort to which many of them go, I believe."

"Probably those who aren't soldiers go there to meet those who are," said Kate. "What fine men those army officers seem to be! I've seen them only at long range—I believe that's a military expression, isn't it?—but they seem so manly and self-possessed; so unlike the little fellows who pass for men in New York."

"Trif," said Fenie, "has often insisted that soldiers have learned the secret of never growing old, and she seems to be right. From the youngest to the oldest, I've found them courteous, agreeable and—and—"

"Deferential?"

"Yes; that is just the word. There's nothing consequential or silly about them, as there is about so many young men and old beaux at home."

"You lucky girl!" exclaimed Kate. "I wonder that your good fortune in meeting such clever fellows hasn't turned your head."

Fenie indulged in a smile that Kate thought quite unusual in a girl so young, a smile which was almost grim, as she replied:

"There's a saying in the family that the Wardlow head never gets entirely off the Wardlow shoulders, and I'm trying to live up to it. Still, I've enjoyed myself greatly in the general company here."

"General company? No man in particular? What a lot of girls whom we both know, would give their heads for your chance. Do you know, Fenie dear, I wouldn't have wondered if by this time you had lost your heart to some one quite competent to care for it."

Fenie looked so astonished, and also so hurt, that Kate called herself a brute. Evidently Harry was safe; the assurance was so exhilarating that Kate lost her own head for a moment or two and began to talk at random.

"What a capital fellow Lieutenant Jermyn is!" she said. "Do you know, it was merely Trixy who introduced him to me, yet he at once made me feel entirely at ease with him."

"Oh, he's charming," replied Fenie. "He's been very kind to Trif and me. He seems to know every one, and he's made us acquainted with many pleasant people. Indeed, I suppose that is the reason Trif is not with us now; she probably is chatting with people whom Jermyn has introduced."

"What a social paragon he must be! I wish he were here now, for I want to ask questions about scores of people whom I am meeting."

"The Admiral could answer them, and quite as well, if he were here," said Fenie innocently.

"The Admiral?"

"Yes." Then Fenie began to tell what a delightful gentleman the old Admiral was. In the meantime Trixy was looking about for the Admiral himself, for it was about the time for the daily inspection of sand-wells and the award of the prize. But Trixy could not see the genial old man anywhere, although she strolled the entire length of the piazza, and then went into the office to ask questions. The Admiral had gone to the club, in the fort, some one said. Well, the fort was but two or three hundred steps away, Trixy knew, for she had been there several times already. She knew, too, where the club was, for Lieutenant Jermyn had taken her there to show her the picture of a distant relation of her mother who had been a soldier.

To the club Trixy went, but an elderly officer whom she met said that the Admiral was not there.

"That's too bad," said Trixy, "'cause some ladies wants him."

Another elderly officer, who was present, admitted that it certainly was too bad, and said that the Admiral would be greatly disappointed.

"Mebbe," said Trixy, a happy thought coming to her mind, "mebbe Lieutenant Jermyn is here."

"He is in one of the section rooms," replied one of the officers.

"He's saying his lessons," added the other "Do you ever have lessons, little girl?"

"Yes, indeed," sighed Trixy. "Some of 'em's awful hard, too, though mamma helps me all she can. But do you mean that a great big man like Lieutenant Jermyn goes to school?"

"Indeed, I do."

"Dear me!" exclaimed the child. Then she thought a moment, and continued:

"Do you suppose his teacher would let him out for a while? Other scholars get let out of school sometimes, when somebody needs to see them very much."

"I think it doubtful," said one of the officers, but the other, with a wink at his companion, said:

"One never knows what can be done until one has tried. Just go over to that door where you see a cat sitting, ask for the teacher, and tell him what you want."

"Thank you," said Trixy, trotting briskly in the direction indicated, while one officer said to the other:

"Colonel, when will you outgrow your fondness for practical jokes?"

"Not while I live, I hope. Besides, where's the harm? Amperthwaite, the instructor of that section, will be cleverer for the remainder of the day, after such an interruption, and the boys will be glad of a moment's truce. I wish I could be there to see and listen."

The door was open, and Jermyn was standing in front of a large blackboard covered with marks which reminded Trixy of the geometrical puzzles which her father sometimes cut from cardboard for her. The instructors and the other officers were looking at the board, and Jermyn was talking, so no one noticed the little girl in the doorway, and Trixy was beginning to feel embarrassed. Suddenly an officer, who had children of his own, attracted attention by coughing violently. Every one looked at him, and he, in turn, looked toward the door.

"Are you the teacher of this school?" asked Trixy of the one officer who sat apart from the others.

"Eh? Oh—yes, what is it?"

"Lieutenant Jermyn, one of your scholars?"

"Er—Mr. Jermyn, do you resent the implication?"

"Not for an instant, Captain."

"Well, little girl, what is it?"

"Oh, only if you'd let him out, there's a couple of ladies who'd like to see him very much; I know they would, because one of them said so."

The only really young lieutenant in the room giggled; the others smiled, and the instructor, after regarding the blackboard intently a moment, said:

"Mr. Jermyn, you may consider yourself excused, if you so desire."

Jermyn emerged with his cap in his hand and more than his customary color in his face. Trixy took his hand, and led him toward the exit nearest the hotel. Looking towards the club, she saw the two officers whom she had met, they having moved their chairs nearer the door that they might observe the proceedings, so she shouted:

"I got him!"

Then each warrior chuckled, although Trixy did not know it, for she was busily explaining to Jermyn why she had come for him, and how hard she had first tried to find the Admiral, and Jermyn told her not to feel the least concern about the interruption, although at the same time he told himself in entire earnest that he wished that Tryphosa Wardlow had never married and become the mother of a child like Trixy, for when would he ever hear the end of the section-room episode?

But Trixy knew nothing of the trouble which she had caused. She prattled without ceasing until she had conducted the officer to her aunt and Miss Trewman, to whom she said:

"Here he is. Now, ask him your questions."

Jermyn soon ceased to feel provoked. One of the duties of a soldier is to endure anything that may lead to desirable ends. It, therefore, came to pass within an hour that Jermyn assured himself that to make himself interesting and useful to two young women like Kate and Fenie was sufficient compensation for any teasing which his comrades might impose in the future. His feelings must have expressed themselves in his face, for a lull in the conversation was improved by Trixy, who said:

"Say, Mr. Jermyn, ain't you glad that I asked your teacher to let you out of school?"

Then Jermyn had to explain; so did Trixy, and the ladies had to feel very uncomfortable.

---

# CHAPTER IX.
## MISPLACED CONFIDENCE.

KATE came within a day or two to enjoy the society of Lieutenant Jermyn so much that she did not hesitate to say so plainly to Fenie. True, she said it half as a test, to be applied to Fenie's own feelings, but as the girl listened without a sign of jealousy, and even looked pleased, Kate was so well satisfied with the situation that she wanted to talk farther on the subject, and with some one more competent to estimate a mature man and gentleman at his true value.

She therefore began to discuss Jermyn with Trif, who was so happy over the change in Fenie's manner that she was quite willing to rejoice and sympathize with any one about anything. Like any other good woman who had been compelled to disappoint a good man, she wished she might see the man made happy by some other good woman, so she wondered whether a match between Jermyn and Kate might not be possible. Her own married life was so happy that she profoundly pitied any other woman who was unmarried yet old enough to know her own mind.

How Trif did long for Phil! If she could see him, only for an hour, to consult with him about this new and delightful idea that had taken possession of her.

Undoubtedly he would agree with her, for he always came to her way of thinking, or she to his, she was not sure which. She had half a mind to telegraph him to run down to the fort for a day or two; she was sure his horrid old firm would not miss him greatly during so short an absence. Then she thought it would be better to write him and ask his advice.

Half wondering which course would be the better, she began a letter, but was interrupted again and again, so at night she was but little further advanced than in the morning. Besides, a series of showers had descended upon Old Point, and Trixy was obliged to remain indoors, and a little girl away from home on a showery day is as restless as a guilty conscience, so Trif finally called herself a heartless mother, and tried to devote herself entirely to her child. Trixy asked only that mamma would write a good long letter for her to papa, and Trif began it, and got well under way, when a waiter came to the room with a message from Fenie, begging Trif to come down at once to see some old friends who had unexpectedly arrived, so poor little Trixy was hurried to bed, where she thought dismally of life's disappointments until she fell asleep.

A little matter like a night's sleep could not make Trixy forget anything upon which she had set her heart. Early the next morning the child begged her mamma to finish that letter to papa, and she reverted to the subject several times during the day. Finally she searched her mother's portfolio for the unfinished letter, and endeavored to complete it herself, in imitation of print, which was the only sort of writing she knew well. She had not learned to use a pen, and the only pencil she could find had a very bad point, so she put both letter and pencil into her pocket, and resolved to bide her time until she could find her mother disengaged.

Once upon the beach, and at her favorite occupation of well-digging, she forgot the letter for two or three hours, but the subject was brought back to her mind by overhearing one of the male guests tell another that he had just received a letter from his little daughter, and that a man never knew how dear his children were until he was separated from them for a few days.

Suddenly the inspector of sand-wells, the cheery old Admiral, hove in view, and Trixy hurried to him and asked:

"You can sharpen lead-pencils, can't you?"

"I could when I was at the Naval Academy," was the modest reply. In a moment Trixy's hand and eyes and head and tongue were working in unison, after the manner of beginners at letter-writing, while the Admiral, standing a little apart, pretended to write something in a memorandum book, but really made a sketch, to be presented to Trif, of the little correspondent as she knelt upon the piazza floor and used a chair as a desk.

"Writin's dreadful hard work," said Trixy, after several moments of effort. "I do wish that mamma—oh, say, Admiral, you can write, can't you? Of course you can—I see you doin' it now. Won't you please finish this letter for me if I tell you what to say? That's the way mamma writes 'em for me—she begun this one. If you do it you needn't pay me five cents the next time my well's the best of the lot, and I guess it's goin' to be the best to-day. Is it a bargain?"

"But, Trixy," replied the Admiral, "I question the propriety of hearing other peoples' family affairs."

"Oh, I don't write no family affairs. This is only a letter to papa."

"Your logic, my dear, is as faultless as your grammar. Still, I'll be your clerk for a few moments."

"All right; I'm very much obliged. First, though, you'd better begin and read what's already wrote, 'cause it's so long since mamma began this letter for me that I can't remember what I told her to say."

"H'm—let me see," said the Admiral, adjusting his glasses. "'Dear Old Papa'——"

"Go on."

The Admiral, who, like most men of affairs, had acquired a way of reading a page at a glance, suddenly looked at Trixy in astonishment. Then he re-read the letter, and said, with a twinkle of his eyes:

"Aren't you rather young to take so much interest in match-making?"

"What's match-makin'?" asked the child, with wondering eyes.

"Oh, you seem to understand the subject very well. The idea of a child planning a marriage between a man and a woman—quite suited to each other though they certainly are—who never met until this week!"

"Who do you mean? Aunt Fee and Harry? Why, they've——"

"No, no—I don't mean them. This is another couple—a lady and an army officer."

"Oh, you mean Mr. Jermyn and Miss Trewman? Why, I don' remember tellin' mamma to write anythin' about them. Come to think of it, though, I said to her, over at guard mount the other day, that 'twould be nice if they got married; but she said 'Sh—h—,' and that means the same thing as don't when mamma says it."

"Yes—to be sure; it used to be so in our family, when I was a boy. But how did this subject get into the letter, if you didn't tell your mother to write it?"

"I'm sure I don't know, unless mamma put it in just for fun. Sometimes she helps me with things to say, when I want to write a real long letter."

"H'm!" The Admiral looked very alert as he recalled customs of his own family when he was a young father. "Trixy, would you mind telling me your father's name—his first name?"

"It's Philip."

"Ah, yes. And is that what your mother usually calls him?"

"Goodness, no! When she says 'Philip,' papa pretends to be awfully scared. Sometimes she calls him Phil, but usually she says 'papa.'"

"Just as I supposed." The Admiral was silent and grave so long that the child timidly asked:

"You don't think it's improper for her to do it, do you?"

"Improper? No, indeed! I'd give half my pay—yes, all of it—to hear my wife call me 'papa' again." Tears came into the veteran's eyes, and Trixy, following home custom regarding such matters, kissed them away, which operation made the Admiral's face as cheery as a sunburst. Nevertheless, the old man did some more thinking, and finally he said:

"I'm such a stupid old fellow that I can't easily finish what some other person has begun. Suppose we destroy this letter, and I begin a new one for you. I'll write one as long as you like, if you'll come into the office, where I can find a desk."

"Oh, good!"

"But about this one which your mother began—suppose we have a secret about it?"

Trixy hesitated; she dearly loved a secret, but of late her secrets had not been as well kept as she would like. Still, she promised, and the new letter was soon under way, and at the top was written, "Dictated to Rear Admiral Allison, retired, by Her Serene Highness the Infanta Trixy." The Admiral put the original and uncompleted letter into his pocket, intending to burn it and destroy the ashes, although what might happen, should there be any enquiries for it, he was sure he did not know; perhaps it might be well for him to hurry off to Washington, or somewhere.

When the new letter was completed Trixy and the Admiral took it to the post-office, and the old man, in endeavoring to impress upon Trixy the advisability of keeping the matter a secret while both of them remained at Old Point, exerted his diplomatic faculties to an extent unparalleled during his entire term of service as an officer. He loathed the idea of teaching duplicity to a child, but in the circumstances it seemed entirely justifiable.

As the day waned, most of the ladies retired to dress for dinner, and Trif, whose conscience had been reproaching her all day for neglect of her husband, to whom she knew her letters were unspeakably welcome, and to whom she dearly loved to write when she chanced to be away from him, determined to finish the letter begun the day before.

"Fenie," she soon said through the door between the rooms, "have you been to my portfolio?"

"No, dear. I've done no writing."

"How strange. I'd begun a letter to Phil, and now I can't find it."

Fenie said something playful about mislaid affection, but Trif did not laugh, for she remembered what she had written. Still, why should she worry? No one but the chambermaid could have been in the room, and she doubted whether colored chambermaids at the South could read. The letter would turn up in the course of time; meanwhile she would write a hasty note to Phil and enclose Trixy's, just as it was, in time for the mail by the evening boat, which would close in a few minutes, and Trixy, who never was specially dressed for dinner, could take the letter down to the office.

The Admiral strolled over to the fort and the club, where he met a semi-public man who was talking to the Commandant about a promising gold "placer" on the Pacific coast which had proved so alluring that he had lost a lot of money in trying to develop it. The Commandant had known of this same placer, for he had been stationed near it at one time; the Admiral also had seen it, for he had been taken to it one day by some men who had hoped to extract some of his savings from him. Lack of water was the trouble, and the Admiral, who had looked carefully over the ground, had devised a plan whereby water might be brought by a tortuous route from a stream several miles distant. When he said this to the semi-public man that person replied:

"Give me your plan, and if it is practicable you shall have a large block of stock, for nothing, in the company I'll organize to work it."

The Admiral quickly took a letter from his pocket and drew on the back of it a plan of the country as he remembered it. Then he consulted Jermyn, who had dropped into the club.

"Very good," said Jermyn, looking at the sketch, "although it might be improved a little, I think. I've done some shooting on that very ground, so I remember it pretty well."

"How fortunate," said the Admiral. "Mr. Blogsham, my friend Jermyn is a good engineer, so he may be of more service than I."

"Good!" said Blogsham. "The better the plan, the more it will be worth to us. There's a block of stock for you too, Mr. Jermyn, if you can make the water within reach."

Jermyn opened the sheet of paper and made another sketch; then he turned the paper over, supposing it might contain some memoranda on the subject, but he saw something that so upset his mind that in the next ten minutes he talked so vaguely about the ground and the water that his own chance of getting any stock in the proposed mine seemed to him very small.

---

# CHAPTER X.
## A SCRAP OF PAPER.

BRUCE JERMYN was as honorable a gentleman as could be found anywhere, but for two or three days and nights he wished he had read farther in that letter upon which he and the Admiral had made their sketches of the surroundings of the placer mine. No one knew better than he the rights and sanctity of private correspondence, but could any man be blamed for wanting to know who it was who was planning to marry him to Kate Trewman?

He could not say that he objected to the lady named in the letter, but who could it be who was charging herself with the conduct of the affair? "Dear old Papa," the letter had begun, and the Admiral being old, and also the possessor of the letter, was undoubtedly the person to whom it was addressed, but who could the writer be? Jermyn knew that the Admiral had at least one daughter, who was a clever woman with some reputation in the service as a match-maker, but she was married and living several hundreds of miles from Old Point.

Perhaps she had arrived, an invalid, and remained in her room; but it was strange that no one mentioned her. Evidently the writer, whoever she might be—for the penmanship was that of a woman—was acquainted with Kate Trewman: in that case her identity might be discovered through Kate, but Jermyn, manly and honest though he was, half felt that he would not again be able to look Kate fully in the face, much less to interrogate her skilfully on so delicate a subject, in which there seemed so much at stake.

All his fears and doubts, however, disappeared like mists before the sun when next he met Kate herself. That estimable young woman was not in the least forward, but she knew how to put at their ease such men as she liked, and she quickly made herself so companionable that Jermyn began to wish that the writer of the letter would go on match-making, and in the greatest of earnest. Still, who on earth, or at Old Point, could she be? The Admiral himself seemed to enter entirely into the spirit of the affair, for he made two or three occasions to speak to Kate and Jermyn together, and to bring out some of the young man's best points; he was as hearty as if he and Jermyn had been boys together, and that sort of thing, from an officer of very high rank to a subaltern, has its effect upon women. Indeed, the old sea-dog was so very familiar that Jermyn almost determined to boldly ask him for another glance at the letter—at least, for a look at the sketches.

But the Admiral's affability and high spirits were partly assumed, for he had a great load of trouble upon his mind. When he reached his room and prepared to burn the tell-tale letter, he could not find the letter itself. What could he have done with it? At times he was very absent-minded; he had been known to go out without his hat, and to search with his right hand for the eye-glasses that were in his left, but he certainly had carried that letter too close to his mind to mislay it. Had he taken any papers from his pocket anywhere? Ha! That sketch of the placer mine.

He hurried back to the fort, but it was not there, nor could he find anyone who had seen it. Probably, the semi-public man, Blogsham, had pocketed the paper, which would have been entirely natural under the circumstances, but Blogsham had already started for Washington.

The Admiral groaned. He remembered that the letter had no signature, so it could not be traced to its writer; but the writer was a woman, and the subject was a woman and an officer, and Blogsham was rather a coarse fellow, and very fond of a practical joke, and if he should chance to know Jermyn——

Know Jermyn? Why, to be sure he knew him! Had not the Admiral himself introduced the Lieutenant, and consulted him about the sketch? Possibly Jermyn himself had the letter; he would ask him. Hence, the Admiral's frequent excuses to speak to Jermyn in Kate's presence, and to finally ask bluntly:

"By the way, Jermyn, do you remember those sketches we made at the club yesterday?"

The young officer suddenly reddened, and the older officer lost heart, although he regained it when Jermyn replied:

"Yes, and I was going to ask you to let me see them once more. Have you them with you?"

The Admiral looked the Lieutenant full in the eye, at which the disappearing flush returned. The Admiral continued:

"I supposed you had it already."

"Not I, I assure you. I left it upon the club table, right at your elbow."

The Admiral suddenly looked so uncomfortable that Jermyn said:

"I sincerely hope you haven't lost it!"

"So do I. I could make the sketch again from memory, but there were some—er—some memoranda on the other side of the sheet which I had intended to preserve; that is, they were not my property, and——"

"Not your property?" Jermyn thought he saw the opportunity for which he was longing.

"No. The letter itself belonged to another person. Do you suppose that Blogsham himself may have kept the sketches for future reference."

"Quite possibly. But Blogsham has returned to Washington."

"So I have heard. I suppose there is nothing left but to write him."

"What a lot of trouble a bit of paper may cause," said Kate, becoming restive during a conversation in which she had no part.

"Yes—yes, indeed," replied the Admiral in a manner so unlike any which Kate had previously seen him display that the young woman began to wonder whether there could be some historic or romantic interest about the bit of paper in which the two men seemed so deeply interested. Everything she had known about gentlemen of the army and navy, until the last two or three days, had been learned from novels and stories, in many of which a bit of paper played an important part. Perhaps there was some romance even about this, and any romance of army and navy would be very interesting to her—could she know it.

An hour later Kate joined Trif and Fenie, with whom sat Harry. Both ladies rallied her about her apparent conquests in both warlike branches of the public service, and Kate finally said that she wished she often could make conquests of such men as Admiral Allison and Lieutenant Jermyn.

"And only think," she added; "I do believe there's some great mystery between the two men. 'Tis none of my affair, of course, but I can't help being curious about it. 'Tis all about some sketches and memoranda of some kind. They talked it over before me without any hesitation, but it was plain to see that there was much more to it than appeared in the conversation."

"Oh," said Fenie, "there seems to be an epidemic of mislaying bits of paper. Trif, here, has been worrying all day about a letter to Phil which she began but didn't finish. I told her it was the easiest thing in the world to write a letter to one's own husband—or ought to be, but she has upset her entire room while searching for that wretched note."

Trif tried to laugh, but she felt very uncomfortable. To change the subject of conversation she called Trixy and examined the child's shoes to see that they were tied, and she set Trixy's hat properly upon her head. Meanwhile Kate continued to talk about the Admiral and the Lieutenant, and their lost sketches and memoranda, and Trixy took part in the conversation by saying that the Admiral was nicer than ever, because he wrote a long letter for her, the day before, to send to her dear papa.

"Trixy!" exclaimed Fenie. "How could you trouble some one not of the family to write a letter for you?"

"Why, him and me is good friends, and mamma began a letter for me, but she put off finishing it, and——"

Trif arose with a start, took the child's hand, and walked away so rapidly that a family woman sitting near by remarked to another family woman that it looked very much as if a certain child was being led to punishment.

"Trixy, dear," asked Trif, as soon as she was well away from the throng, "how did the Admiral come to write that letter for you?"

"Why," explained Trixy, "I wanted that letter finished, you know, 'cause I promised papa when we started down here that I wouldn't neglect him, so I tried to finish it myself, but 'twas dreadful hard work for me, 'cause the bottom of a chair isn't a very good table, so I asked the Admiral to finish it for me."

"But the letter itself—where did you get it? Where is it now?"

"Got it out of your portfolio, where you put it when you stopped writin' it."

"You dreadful child! The letter I began for you I sent to your father, just as it was, and the one you took from my portfolio was my own."

Trixy had often been called dreadful; the word was in common use in the family, although it was generally accompanied by a smile and a kiss. Now, however, there was no such demonstration. Trif looked so stern that Trixy began to cry, and, as the mother's expression did not relax, the child was soon crying industriously, while Fenie, who had been looking on from a distance wondering what was going on, and indignant that any one—except, perhaps, herself—should do anything to make the dear child uncomfortable, hurried to the rescue.

"I think you're making a great fuss about a very small matter," said Fenie, with the firm conviction and superior sense peculiar to very young women. "I don't see anything to it that you can complain of, except that Trixy got the wrong letter finished. I'm sure you can have written nothing which was unfit for your husband to receive."

"But suppose the Admiral has chanced to read what was already written?"

"Suppose he did? What then?"

"He knows Jermyn, and—oh, oh, oh!"

Trif's manner was so tragical that Fenie was mystified! What could it all mean? It couldn't be that her sister had become too fond of Jermyn, and had any foolishness to confess to her husband; but, if not, what was there dreadful about the fact that the Admiral knew Jermyn?

In the meantime, Trixy had followed the custom of children in general in such cases, which is to get away from the scene of trouble as soon as possible. Chancing to meet the Admiral himself, she abruptly said to him:

"Say, mamma knows all about that letter. I didn't tell her nothin'—she just guessed it."

"Whew!" exclaimed the old man. Then he looked as thoughtful and anxious for a moment as if he were taking a fleet into action, and he said, half to himself, "I must take the night-boat for Washington. I hope Blogsham may still be there. I must beg you to excuse me, Trixy."

The Admiral hurried into the hotel, Trixy following him as far as she could. At the other front of the house she met Jermyn, followed by a servant with a portmanteau.

"Good bye, little girl," said the officer. "I shall be back in a couple of days. A friend of mine is about to run up to Washington with one of the government boats, and I'm going with him. Please remember me to your mother and aunt, and to Miss Trewman."

"What! you goin' to Washin'ton too. So's the Admiral."

Jermyn stared wonderingly, and the last of him that Trixy saw to remember was a face which seemed one great frown.

# CHAPTER XI.
## OFF THE SCENT.

THE Admiral and the Lieutenant met face to face in the Army and Navy Club at Washington, and each looked as if he were a rogue about to tumble into the clutches of the law. After a moment of mute inquiry of each other's faces the Admiral asked:

"Jermyn, how on earth did you reach here? I thought I left you at Fort Monroe?"

"And I," said Jermyn, "supposed I had left you at Old Point, when I suddenly ran up here on a matter of personal business."

"Ah! Trying to be transferred to some other branch of the service, where there's more chance of promotion? Well, I can't blame you. In time of peace a man must wait a long while for his just deserts, and in time of war he may be killed before they can reach him. 'Tis a queer world."

"It certainly is, or some things in it are very queer."

"Excuse a plain question, please. That letter upon which you and I sketched a day or two ago at the club—was it——"

"Bless my soul, Jermyn, is that letter on your mind too? My dear boy, my sole purpose in hurrying off to Washington last night was to recover that letter. I can't imagine where it is unless our enterprising friend Blogsham took it with him."

"You knew its contents?"

"Yes—unfortunately for my peace of mind since I was asked to read it. But you——"

"I," said Jermyn, "glanced at it, supposing it to be memoranda about the property you were discussing; I had no idea that it could be a private letter. You will understand why I would like to know something further about it, principally to save one woman, possibly two women, from great mortification should the letter itself fall into the wrong hands."

"Possibly two women?" repeated the Admiral. "Do you mean to say that you don't know who the writer was?"

"I've not the slightest idea."

The Admiral knocked the ashes from his cigar, and took several puffs, regarding Jermyn quizzically in the meantime, before he replied:

"Dear boy, you've a powerful friend at court, if your interests are what they might be. The writer of the letter, who I assure you is not a member of my own family, was writing to some one to whom she has an entire right to open her mind freely. If that little scamp Trixy hadn't—"

"Aha! Mrs. Highwood was the writer, eh?"

Jermyn seemed greatly relieved by his discovery, but the Admiral said indignantly:

"Jermyn, you ought to be ashamed of yourself for entrapping an old friend in that way— you really ought. Beside, you ought to be grateful that so good a woman is taking so great interest in you. As to the lady whom she named, any man alive ought to be glad of an opportunity to make love to her, and marry her, but if you don't think so———"

"I fully agree with you, Admiral, but if the lady herself chances to hear of it—if our mining acquaintance chances to be one of the fellows who sees a joke in everything, and doesn't care to whom he tells it, and if he has the letter, and shows it to mutual acquaintances—well, you know how a story gains by being passed from man to man."

"Quite true, quite true," assented the Admiral with a groan. "We must look the fellow up, and at once. Bless me! To think that all this trouble came about through a child asking me to finish a letter to her father. If I could lay my hands upon that youngster at this moment I'd—I'd———"

"You'd probably romp with her as pleasantly as if nothing had occurred."

"Yes, probably."

Trixy would have been glad of some one to romp with at that moment, for she was very unhappy. Her mother seemed utterly wretched; at other times when Trif was troubled in mind, Trixy had been quick to note it and to be very affectionate, and had been so successful as to be called her mamma's greatest comfort. Fenie, too, was miserable, for Trif had told her what was in the missing letter, and Fenie was sure that if the letter itself fell into improper hands, and Kate should hear about it, and learn who was the writer, there would be another danger of coolness between the two families, for Kate was too proud to endure any interference with her own affairs. Fenie had her own reasons for objecting to any such trouble, for she was very happy with Harry; there had been no talk of love, but none was necessary. Young people have ways of understanding each other quite independently of words; do not even deaf mutes fall in love?

Now, however, even Fenie's pleasant chats with Harry might have to be suspended, for Trif was in such abject fear and mortification that she would scarcely leave her room, and Fenie did not like to appear entirely unattended and unwatched by her sister. No one would talk if she were seen with Kate and Harry together, but Fenie herself, like Trif, had imagined all sorts of possible and impossible ways by which that dreadful letter, or some garbled report of it, might reach Kate.

So, the sisters sat in their room, and feared, and felt like a couple of criminals to whom the worst might happen. They exchanged forebodings, all of which were overheard by Trixy, who received a reproachful look with each, and did quite a lot of silent weeping on her own account, and neither her mother nor her aunt dried her eyes with kisses, as they usually did at home after she had done something wrong, and repented.

But the kind power that looks after children and fools came finally to Trixy's relief, for Trif suddenly said:

"Surely the mail is distributed by this time, and I can have at least the consolation of a letter from dear Phil. Trixy, go down to the office and ask for letters for our room."

Trixy flew away like a bird from an opened cage, and no sooner did she reach the lower floor than she dashed through one of the exits to the beach. How delicious the sunlight was, after part of a morning in a half-darkened room!—the child felt as if she were bathing in it. And the beach, too, with its long edging of smooth, hard sand,—she must have just one run on it, from pier to pier, and back again.

It was a merry run, but it put her out of breath, so she threw herself down upon the sand to rest for a moment, and the warm-hearted sand welcomed her so pleasantly that she waited a moment longer, and then another, and soon she began to doze, for contemplation of other people's troubles had wearied her early in the day.

Suddenly she was roused by the touch of a parasol-tip. Looking up, she saw Kate Trewman, who said:

"Trixy, is your family ill, or merely sleepy? They usually are down early to breakfast."

"Oh, they're bothered. My what a fuss! Say, you won't get angry at 'em, will you?"

"Not I! Why should I? I shall be very sorry, though, if they remain in their rooms all morning, for I miss them greatly. I don't find any of my acquaintances this morning."

"Don't you? Well, I know where one of 'em is. He's gone to Washin'ton, Lieutenant Jermyn has."

Kate said nothing in reply, but Trixy exclaimed, "Goodness gracious! How bad you do feel about it! So do I. But he's comin' back—comin' to-morrow, 'cause he said he'd be gone only a couple of days. Oh, how quick you do get glad again!"

Kate abruptly turned her face aside, hid it in her parasol, and thanked herself that she had no little sister or niece, to be always observing her—and so exasperatingly correctly, too! At that moment her brother joined her, and asked Trixy if she would give his card, on which he had pencilled a line or two, to her Aunt Fee. This reminded Trixy that she had been sent for the mail, so she danced off in the direction of the office, while Harry and Kate walked to and fro, and talked of everything but what was uppermost in their minds.

Trixy found additional causes of detention. The mail was late, and a throng of people were at the desk awaiting the distribution, so Trixy went to the front door to look at the flowers which colored people brought every morning to sell to the guests. Then she strolled toward the fort, to look at an old colored beggar, whose raggedness was so picturesque that it fascinated her. As she stood staring at him, a servant from the fort accosted her with,

"Little girl, you know Adm'ral All'son, don't you?—the old gen'leman that bosses all you young ones when you digs sand-wells?"

"Of course I do; he's one of my best friends."

"Well, I've got lots to do this mornin', an' I don't see how I'm goin' to git through. Don't you want to give this letter to him for me?"

"Certainly."

"You won't forget it, will you?"

"Oh, no; I'm not of the forgettin' kind." And Trixy took the letter, forgetting for the moment that the Admiral had gone to Washington. Then she hurried back to the hotel, got the mail, and went into her mother's room, saying:

"Let me open the letters for you, won't you, like papa does?"

"Yes, but do it quickly," said Trif, first selecting one from her husband, which she quickly read and re-read. Then she took the others, after Trixy had cut the ends of the envelopes, and glanced over them, commenting as she read:

"H'm—nothing unusual. Mrs. Poynce's cards, the Misses Brimling's tea, on Thursday next—I shall be sorry to miss it; invitation to a spring opening, and—oh!"

Trif fell back in her chair, as if in a faint. Fenie hurried to her, exclaiming:

"Trif, dear! What is the matter? Speak to me, quick!"

"That letter! That awful letter that I began for Trixy! Here it is!"

"Dear me! Where could it have come from?"

"I can't imagine. Why—the envelope is addressed to Admiral Allison! How could it have got among our letters?"

"Oh," said Trixy, as excited as anyone, "a man gave me the letter, a few minutes ago, to give to the Admiral, and I forgot all about it, and I've gone and cut the end of it, with the others!"

"But who can it have come from?" persisted Trif, looking into the envelope. "There is nothing else with it, and some one had drawn pictures on blank parts of the sheets."

"He must have lent it to someone, who is returning it to him," suggested Fenie.

"I've always supposed naval officers the soul of honor?" sighed Trif.

"Won't you give me the drawing on the back of it for my scrap-book, mamma?" asked Trixy. No objection being made, Trixy tore the Admiral's sketch of the gold placer and vicinity from the sheet, and pasted it into a fearfully and wonderfully made book of pictures, which she had brought from home. She looked at Jermyn's sketch a moment, thought it very like the other, and cast it aside. Her mother picked it up, read the page which she had written, and then she and Fenie devised wildly improbable theories of the history of the letter. The conclusion finally reached, greatly though they regretted it, was that the letter had been lent by the Admiral to someone in the fort, with the impression that there was some fun in it. If army and navy officers saw jokes in such things, of course Jermyn would soon hear of the letter itself, to his great discomfort; for the sisters agreed that he was too much of a gentleman to laugh over such a matter. Suddenly Fenie exclaimed:

"There's something more dreadful still. You'll have to return the letter to the Admiral."

"Never," Trif replied. "I shall mail it to Phil this very afternoon." Suiting the action to the word she enclosed it in an envelope, addressed it, and affixed a stamp to it.

"But," remonstrated Fenie, "when the Admiral returns he will want to know where the letter is, and he will speak to the man to whom he lent it, and the man will say that he sent it back, and the servant will be questioned and say he gave it to Trixy, and then—"

"Probably the messenger doesn't know Trixy by sight or name," said Trif.

"Oh, he knows me well enough," said Trixy. "He's servant to somebody in the fort, and the somebody's little girls play with me on the beach sometimes, and he comes for 'em at dinnertime and lunch time."

"I see nothing to be done, then," said Trif, "but for me to return to New York at once. We certainly owe neither courtesy nor explanation to the Admiral, whom we won't have the embarrassment of meeting if we are not here. Why, Fenie, you're crying. What is the matter, dear?"

"I should think you might know, without asking," sobbed the girl, "you, who have been in love, and——"

"You poor, dear child. Your sister is a thoughtless, heartless brute. Still, the Trewmans themselves will not remain here long; Kate said they had dropped over here only for a day or two, to see what the place——"

"Oh, that reminds me," said Trixy. "Harry gave me a card for Aunt Fee a few minutes ago. Here it is."

Fenie read the message on the card, and looked pleased, although she said:

"Oh, Harry thinks they too will have to go to New York, this very evening. He—that is, Kate, is waiting for me down stairs. You won't mind my joining her, will you? She does so dislike to be kept waiting."

# CHAPTER XII.
## THE SEARCH PARTY.

THE Admiral and the Lieutenant searched Washington quickly yet thoroughly, for the man who was supposed to have the fateful letter in his possession was prominent enough to have his every movement observed and recorded by the newspapers and discussed by the clubs. No one at Washington had seen him or heard of him since his departure for Old Point.

"Let us hope, dear boy," said the Admiral, as the disappointed and weary men lunched together, "that he has gone to the Pacific Coast to develop that placer, for no one out there will take any interest in that unfortunate note."

"I should be glad to hope so," Jermyn replied, "but suppose that he has gone to New York? That is his usual base of operations, and should he have the letter, and meet in New York some one who knows me, it would be just like him to show the letter and talk about it."

"I shall at once go to New York, find him, if he is there, and stop him," said the Admiral.

"But, Admiral——"

"But me no buts, my dear boy. I assure you that if it weren't for my humiliation at having been a thoughtless old donkey I'd enjoy the job almost as well as if I were in active service and in chase of an enemy. A chase will do me good—keep me from rusting, you know."

"But, Admiral, you were having a delightful time at the Point; there was a host of your friends and old comrades there, and they will soon be going away. I've three days' leave of absence, and no farther use to make of it here. Still more, I'm the party most at interest, you know."

"But I'm the one most at fault," persisted the Admiral. It was finally agreed that there should be a division of labor, the Admiral returning to Old Point, where he might learn from some one the destination of the supposed custodian of the letter, while Jermyn should hurry to New York, where it would not be very hard to find the wanted man if he were there.

The Lieutenant had not been long in the metropolis before he learned that even a man known throughout the nation could not easily be found in a city as large as New York. He first went to a club where some old acquaintances were so glad to see him that he had hard work in getting away from them. They all knew by name and reputation the man he was looking for and congratulated Jermyn on having any excuse for seeing a man who had made the fortunes of a dozen other men while making his own, but of the man's whereabouts they were as ignorant as Jermyn himself. Then Jermyn made the rounds of the principal hotels, but he found that their number had trebled since his own period of duty near New York, ten years earlier, and he began to think seriously of applying for an additional leave of absence for three days, on the ground of urgent and unexpected personal business.

He was so weary at the end of a single day's search, that he had not the heart to go to club or theatre, so he dined dismally and alone at Delmonico's, and then sauntered over to Madison Square, dropped upon a bench, and blamed the trees for not being as fully in leaf as those he had left in the South, three hundred miles away.

Suddenly a gentleman arose from a bench near by, walked to and fro two or three times, stopped in front of the lonely officer, and said:

"I beg your pardon, sir, but aren't you Lieutenant Jermyn, of the artillery service?"

"Mr. Highwood!" exclaimed Jermyn, springing to his feet, and extending his hand, "this is rare good fortune for me."

"And for me," replied Phil; "for you are the only person I know who has seen my family within a week, and I'm as lonesome without that family as you can ever have been at the smallest post you ever served at. Take pity on a poor fellow, and tell me all you can."

"Your loss is their gain," said Jermyn, when both had seated themselves. "I never saw Mrs. Highwood looking better. As for your daughter, she is one of the most engaging young women I ever met, except her mother, whom she greatly resembles. Miss Wardlow, whom Mrs. Highwood told me was in poor health when she left New York, is simply radiant; she is the beauty of the Point, although she doesn't seem to know it. They all talk of you a great deal; to hear Miss Trixy is to believe you the only man on the face of the earth."

"Bless her!" said Phil. "By the way, there are some neighbors of ours there, I believe—the Trewmans. Have you chanced to meet them?"

As he asked this question, Phil looked sidewise at his companion, and was sure, despite the uncertain light of an electric lamp, that the officer's face colored a little. But Jermyn replied, in his ordinary tone:

"Delightful people—delightful! By the way, I've a suspicion that you're in danger of losing your sister-in-law; at least as a member of your immediate family. Mr. Trewman is devotion itself, and although the young lady has many admirers, Mr. Trewman seems to be the favored one."

"Ah! Well, I don't know that either of them could do better. They are already very well acquainted, and Fenie is quite fond of Harry's sister, whom I imagine does not disapprove of the match."

Jermyn did not reply, so Highwood continued to talk about the Trewmans, and particularly about Kate; and Jermyn replied briefly, from time to time, speaking of Kate so admiringly, yet guardedly, that Phil began to wonder whether the officer had not been making love with traditional military haste, and had his suit discouraged. Being too good a man to persist in talking of a subject regarding which his companion felt any reason for restraint, he hastened to change the subject, and the two men were soon engaged in general chat. Phil soon asked:

"How long shall you remain in the city, Mr. Jermyn? Or perhaps you are to be on duty here?"

"Only on personal business, which may take three or four days."

"Good! I'll try to see that your spare time passes pleasantly. Several new military pictures are to be exhibited at my club, and I'll be glad to have you see them, if you find the time. I received several invitations in blank to-day; let me give you one."

Phil drew some papers from his pocket, and began to search for the invitations, holding his letters and other papers so that the light might strike them fairly. Suddenly he was conscious of a start. He looked up inquiringly, and saw Jermyn gazing intently at a letter which Phil held in his hand.

"Ah?" said Phil, quickly, "apparently you recognize this picture. Perhaps you can tell me what it is. It has puzzled me not a little, for it is on the back of a letter from my wife, who sketches a little, but this sketch is not in her style."

"It reminds me," replied Jermyn deliberately, and with a visible affectation of carelessness, "of a bit of far Western scenery, which I used to know quite well, having been there on duty."

Jermyn wished he could be alone a moment—wished he were a boy again, and in the centre of a great field or forest, where he could give a great, joyous shout. That missing letter! It had reached rightful hands at last—but how? He must telegraph the Admiral at once; how delighted the dear old fellow would be! Still, how in the name of all that was mysterious, had the tormenting screed found its way to the man to whom it was written? There was no address, nor even name, on the paper when he glanced at it in the fort, so the man for whom the sketches were made could not have known to whom it belonged.

"When did you receive the sketch, Mr. Highwood?" Jermyn asked. "Perhaps there is an artist at the Point, of whom I have not heard."

"It came this morning," Phil replied, hoping at the same time that his face was not telling of what was running in his mind. What would the man beside him think if he could know the contents of the letter? "It was evidently begun on one day and finished on another, for there are hints in it of a story which Mrs. Highwood will tell me when she reaches home. She is a dear, good wife, but she does hate to write a longer letter than is absolutely necessary."

"I wonder that she gets time to write at all," said Jermyn, "for she is in great demand. She has probably written you that she has met several old acquaintances; nice people from everywhere seem to gravitate toward Old Point."

Then Jermyn lapsed into such deep thought about that letter, and the ways in which it might have got back to its owner, that he almost forgot that he was not alone.

"What can be the matter with the fellow?" wondered Highwood. "If Trif were almost any other woman in the world, I would think that there was some mystery in which she and he were mutually interested. I shall write her before I sleep, and ask her all about it; I don't know when in my life I've been so curious about anything."

"By the way, Mr. Highwood," said Jermyn, with the idea that he might get some clue to the course of the letter, "I ought to tell you that your daughter is flirting most outrageously with one of the finest gentlemen at the Point. He is a retired admiral—Allison—perhaps you may have heard his name?"

"Heard of him?" echoed Phil; "all Americans are proud of him. That isn't all; he acted as Trixy's amanuensis a day or two ago, and I suspect that some of the funny things in the letter which I received were devised by him; I've played that trick myself with Trixy's missives at times."

"Possibly you are right," was the reply, "for he is as full of fun as any one I know."

"Perhaps the Admiral was the artist who drew that sketch?" Phil suggested.

"H'm! No, I think not. I know his style."

"Would you mind asking him on your return?" persisted Phil.

"Not in the least. I probably shall see him to-morrow night, and——"

"What! Is he, too, coming to New York?"

"Oh, no. He had intended to come, but I came instead."

"But how can you see him to-morrow night?"

"Easily. I shall take the morning train, which will get me to the fort by nine o'clock, at the latest."

"Excuse me, but didn't I understand you to say that you would be here several days?"

"Er—I had intended to remain several days, but I've had the bad manners to think occasionally about business while we've been talking, and something has come to mind which will compel my return at once. 'Tis a mean thing to admit, but greatly though I've enjoyed meeting you here—and I assure you that I never in my life met any one more gladly—my personal business, which brought me here, has persisted in popping into my head. I left the fort in great haste—so great that I left some of the threads of my business behind me."

Phil Highwood was a gentleman, so he detested any one who pried into the private affairs of others, but for a moment he wished himself a mind-reader, or hypnotist, or something of the sort. Meanwhile, Jermyn, who felt that he must be alone, said:

"Won't you honor me with some message to your family?"

"Tell my wife to write me who drew that sketch, please?"

The two men separated, and Jermyn hurried up Broadway, feeling younger than he had at any time in the last ten years.

# CHAPTER XIII.
## A PLAN OF CAMPAIGN.

DURING his trip from Washington back to Old Point, the Admiral promised himself several times that he never again would endeavor to complete a letter begun by any other person. He also resolved that, on reaching the hotel, he would make a full and frank explanation to Mrs. Highwood, and would offer to make reparation, so far as was in his power, by acting as an ally in the lady's campaign to effect the capture of Kate and Jermyn by each other. He had done some discreet match-making in his time, so he felt justified in assuring Trif that there were ways in which he might be useful.

The matter was arranged to his entire satisfaction, in his own mind, before he fell asleep, but somehow plans made at night, even by persons of much experience and shrewdness, do not always stand the test of daylight. He had been at the hotel two or three hours when he came face to face with Trif; the lady passed him with half-averted face and the slightest possible inclination of the head. The Admiral felt indignant, and not a little angry. Could it be possible that matters had gone from bad to worse during his absence? There was no pluckier man in the service than Rear-Admiral Allison, retired, but for a moment or two the old gentleman was tempted to leave Old Point at once.

Soon, however, he regained his courage and did some cautious reconnoitering. He made the tour of the office, parlors, piazzas, and beach, and his search was finally rewarded by a glimpse of Kate and her brother, strolling to and fro on the pier. Had any harm, any publicity, come of that enraging letter, Kate would probably be more angry than any one else, and the first person to whom he should explain, so with a sinking feeling, such as he had not experienced since the time he first went into action, he strode down the pier. Miss Trewman was not above the average height of women, but she looked very tall and imperious as the Admiral marched forward to his fate, whatever it might be. Suddenly Kate saw him and seemed surprised; then she stepped quickly toward him. The old gentleman felt himself turning pale, but Kate gave him a smile which made him as happy, he afterward told her, as if he were again a young man, and she his sweetheart.

"Oh, Admiral!" exclaimed Kate, "how glad I am to see you back! Everything here has been stupid since you went away. Has anything gone wrong with— with any one?"

"Not with you, I'm sure, if looks are any indication. How is Mrs. Highwood and her sister, and Trixy?"

"Trif appears to be ill, although she says nothing is the matter with her. Fenie is worrying about Trif, and poor little Trixy seems in trouble about something."

"H'm," said the Admiral, looking grave.

"Something is the matter," exclaimed Kate. "I see it in your face. Do tell me what it is. The Highwoods are old friends of ours, and if I could know of anything that should be done for any of them I would be very grateful."

"Really, I know of nothing. Lieutenant Jermyn———"

Kate's face colored, and the Admiral's keen eyes twinkled as their owner continued:

"Jermyn and I ran up to Washington a night or two ago on business, so I've heard of nothing that has occurred here since then. Jermyn wasn't able to return with me, but he won't remain long away; indeed, I know he has the best of reasons for wishing himself back again."

Again Kate blushed, which was exactly what the Admiral hoped would be the result of his speech. Still, the girl seemed suspicious about something, so the old gentleman began to talk of something else with his customary ability. While he was talking, a waiter from the hotel approached and handed him a telegram.

"Kindly excuse me a moment?" said the Admiral, adjusting his glasses and opening the envelope. Then he glanced at the dispatch and exclaimed:

"Good!"

"May we congratulate you upon something?—the thanks of Congress, or a new war?"

"Better still. The business upon which Jermyn and I went North has been satisfactorily concluded. Will you kindly excuse me a few moments, until I can write a letter? I will do myself the honor of rejoining you."

"There is probably some secret government business in the hands of the Admiral and the Lieutenant," suggested Harry.

"Secret nonsense! It is something which is mixed up in some way with the strange manner of Trif and Fenie, and the Admiral must simply tell what it is."

Meanwhile the old gentleman was re-reading the dispatch, which was as follows:

"That letter is in proper hands. Jermyn."

"Proper hands! Proper hands!" repeated the Admiral to himself. "Evidently that means his own hands. Fine fellow! He deserves the girl, if only for the pains he has taken to keep her name from being used publicly. How I wish I might tell her the whole story! Still, if they continue to like each other, my time will come. I think that I ought now to be able to make my peace with Mrs. Highwood. I need merely to repeat to her Jermyn's own words, and crave the privilege of age to laugh with her over a matter entirely to her credit."

Within five minutes the Admiral had dispatched a note to Trif, who languidly opened it and then suddenly dropped her languor and called Fenie, to whom she said:

"What can the man mean? There can be but one letter that the man refers to—the one which Trixy gave him, and which she got back so strangely, and I sent on to Phil, promising that I would tell him something about it when I reached home. Phil don't know the Admiral, so I can't make sense out of the matter. It isn't possible that Trixy is making any more trouble with letters?"

"Don't be silly!" replied Fenie. "What did the poor child know about the matter?"

"Oh, I'm afraid she overheard us wondering whether the letter ought not go back to the Admiral, because whoever sent it back to him would be sure to ask whether he received it, and—Trixy, where are you? Have you opened any of my letters?"

"No, mamma; really and truly I haven't," was the indignant reply.

"Oh," said Trif, "I do wish I could find out what it means. If I don't know pretty soon I'm sure I shall go insane."

Fenie made haste to be sisterly and soothing, and Trixy improved the opportunity to escape from the room. She hurried down to the piazza, asked every one she knew whether they had seen the Admiral, and finally she found him talking with Kate and Harry. She did not wait for a lull in the conversation; she stopped before him and interrupted with——

"Say, you don't want my dear mamma to go insane, do you?"

"Bless me, no! What do you mean, child?"

"Why, she says she's goin' to go insane if she doesn't find out all about that letter."

The Admiral looked embarrassed; then he said: "You will kindly excuse me a few moments, Miss Trewman," and quickly led Trixy aside, while Kate told her brother that she, too, would go insane, she thought, unless she could know what dreadful mystery was in the air.

The Admiral made haste to send the child to her mother with the request that Mrs. Highwood would kindly grant an interview in one of the less frequented parlors, which he designated. Within a few moments he was talking earnestly with Trif and trying to convince her that the troublesome letter was in Jermyn's possession.

Then he lost his mental balance for a moment or two, for Trif assured him that beyond doubt he was mistaken, for she had mailed the letter to her husband, who by no possibility could have given it to any one.

The Admiral made haste to put Jermyn's dispatch in evidence, and again Trif was mystified, for although she knew that her husband and Jermyn were acquainted it seemed scarcely possible that Jermyn had called on Phil while on the errand which the old gentleman had carefully explained, with the effect of making her appear his admirer once more. The Admiral tried to reason it out, and offered the suggestion that perhaps her husband had done, in a blunt, straightforward way, as most honest men are likely to do, exactly what she would have wished him to do.

"You may depend upon it, my dear madam, that what I have suggested is exactly what has happened. They have met, probably by accident; your husband has quizzed Jermyn about Miss Trewman, Jermyn has admitted his interest in the lady; your husband has expressed his interest and volunteered his assistance, and to show that you also were interested he has given Jermyn—not the letter, but some word which has satisfied the young man that the letter reached its proper destination."

"I hope you are right," said Trif, "and for the rest———"

"For the rest," continued the Admiral, "can't you and I afford to laugh the matter away? I've honestly explained how innocently I was led to read what Trixy brought me. The letter itself did great credit to your head and heart; the young people are singularly suited to each other, and there is no probability that Miss Trewman will ever hear anything about it, for the manner in which the letter was returned to you shows that it was forwarded to me by some one who was present when I thoughtlessly sketched upon it. As no one but army officers, and one other person, was there, it is probable that some officer returned it, and army officers are gentlemen; none of them would repeat what he chanced to see in a private letter, particularly as his most natural conclusion would be that the letter, having been seen in my possession, had been written to me by some member of my own family."

Trif felt much better, and finally pleased the old gentleman by laughing and accepting him as an ally, and also by accepting his invitation to walk upon the beach and take some delicious air, of which, through his own carelessness, she had recently been deprived.

Trif was as happy as an innocent soul released suddenly from prison, and the Admiral, his own honest heart relieved of its burden, was chatting cheerily and delightfully, when both met Trixy, who looked as if something dreadful had befallen her.

"My dear little darling, what is the matter?" asked Trif.

"She said she wondered if you'd been doin' anythin' dreadful, 'cause I said you might get insane."

"She? Whom do you mean?"

"Why, Miss Trewman. And I just told her, 'no, indeed,' and she said it was too bad that a letter should make anybody such a lot of trouble, and I told her that the letter wasn't about you at all, but was all about her, 'cause I heard you and Aunt Fee talkin' about it. Then she looked awful cross, and I told her she needn't, 'cause 'twas about somethin' nice for her."

"Trixy, dear, how much more did you tell her?"

"Nothin', mamma. You don't think I'm goin' to tell things to people, after all you've said to me about not doin' it, do you? I only told her that you and papa was arrangin' a real nice s'prise for her, and she asked if the Admiral was helpin' do it, 'cause he seemed to be. But I didn't tell her nothin' about it—really I didn't."

# CHAPTER XIV.
## THE COURSE OF TRUE LOVE.

JERMYN hurried back to his post of duty with such mental rapidity that neither train nor steamer could keep pace with him. He told himself that he was a fool; that he had not known Kate Trewman a week, and that in the first half of that same week he had imagined himself in love with Trif's sister, yet, after everything that he could say against himself, the fact remained that he was so interested in Miss Trewman that he had all sorts of fears as to what might happen to his prospects during his absence.

He told himself that probably she was already engaged to some other man, for such women were so scarce that he could not understand how one of them had thus far escaped matrimony. He also reminded himself that he had been admiring fine women all his life, and that quite a number of them had married other men, generally before he had been able to interest them in himself. Still, what did that prove? Merely, that good men, like great men, thought alike. He would not make a fool of himself; he really wasn't in love, but he certainly would endeavor to become better acquainted with Miss Trewman, and if she were not already promised to another, he would make her his own, unless she objected.

The first thing necessary, however, upon reaching Old Point, was to report to his superior officer. He, therefore, hurried to the fort; then, on his way back to the hotel, he dropped into the club, merely to see who was there, or had been there, and in an instant he was buttonholed by the Admiral, who drew him aside, and said:

"Tell me all about it! Facts first and explanations afterward."

"There's nothing to tell," Jermyn replied, "except that Mr. Highwood has that exasperating letter. Is there anything new at the hotel?"

"Nothing except that Miss Trixy—what a genius for mischief that child has!—Trixy has made a coolness in some way between the Highwoods and Trewmans. Miss Trewman acts all the while as if there was something on her mind that was worth being indignant about, and I assure you that the entire situation is extremely uncomfortable for a certain old gentleman who wishes nothing but the best to all parties."

Jermyn frowned and said:

"I suppose the sooner I try to find out what it all is about, the better it will be for my peace of mind."

"Be very careful, I beg of you, my dear boy," exclaimed the Admiral, as Jermyn started away. "Miss Trewman is a most estimable young woman, but she has a mind of her own."

"So much the better. It probably will teach her to have proper respect for other peoples' minds."

"But mayn't I suggest———"

"Perhaps—when I return."

With that reply, the Admiral looked miserable and undecided, and he finally persuaded some one to join him at a game of checkers, which to that day he had thought the last refuge of an adult mind which also was diseased.

Jermyn hurried toward the hotel, determined to take whatever misfortune might come to him, rather than be annoyed by more accidents. As to Trixy—Jermyn had always liked children, and years before, he had made a reputation on a western bound train, and afterward in the service, by caring all night for a fretful child so that the infant's mother might get some needed rest. He wished he might have charge of Trixy for a few days; she was Trif's child, and Trif was to him the ideal woman, and it was impossible that the child should not have inherited some of her mother's estimable qualities; but if Trixy had been making new and unexpected trouble for him, he wished there might be excuse for putting her into the most remote casemate of the fort, locking the door, and losing the key.

As he thought and fretted, he entered the hotel and made his way through office and parlor toward the ball-room, where every one who did not dance congregated to look at every one who did. He nodded to several acquaintances, but his thoughts were entirely about Trixy until he was recalled to better command of himself by the sound of a well-remembered voice:

"Oh, Mr. Jermyn! What an unexpected pleasure! We were told that you would be away several days."

"I am glad to say that I am not so unfortunate," Jermyn replied.

"Hello, Mr. Jermyn," piped a small voice from somewhere behind Miss Trewman, and then the young man saw Trixy, looking as innocent and confiding as if nothing whatever had happened which could trouble her mind or her conscience.

"Trixy!" exclaimed Jermyn, advancing menacingly upon the child. "I met your father yesterday, and he told me to give you a thorough shaking for him"—here he picked up the child and acted according to Phil's orders—"and," he continued, "I suppose he would have sent you a kiss also if I hadn't left him in haste, so I'll give you one on suspicion."

"That is a very interesting child," said Kate, as Trixy hurried away to find her mother and aunt and report Jermyn's return, "but I do think she can make more trouble than any other child I ever heard of."

"Such offences must be condoned, I suppose," replied Jermyn, too happily surprised by his reception to harbor ill-will against any one.

"What a forgiving mood—for a soldier!" said Kate, who imagined Jermyn knew something of the mystery she was trying to fathom.

"Soldiers are often compelled to learn that those who do most harm mean least," Jermyn replied. "But what has the child been doing since I went away?"

"I've not the slightest idea. Perhaps she has done nothing, but she has excited my curiosity greatly, through some references to myself." Then Kate looked enquiringly into Jermyn's eyes, and the young man was so delighted to be looked at by her in any way that he met her gaze unflinchingly, although respectfully, and finally overcame it, and Kate, wishing to change the subject of conversation, murmured something about the heat of the room.

"Let us escape from it," suggested Jermyn, "and join Mrs. Highwood and her sister. Probably they are on the piazza, for I saw Trixy disappear in that direction."

No one who hasn't tried it knows how hard it is to find any one on a crowded piazza a quarter of a mile long, and after sunset too. Success is still more difficult when the searchers have something else to concern their minds and eyes. Jermyn and Kate were clever talkers, and neither of them had often found company so agreeable, so they passed and repassed Trif and Fenie several times without seeing them, and Trif smiled archly, and Fenie gave her a warning pinch, for Harry was with them.

Harry himself was no fool, and as the ladies themselves suddenly lapsed into comparative silence he remembered that his sister frequently reminded him that ladies had affairs of their own to talk about, so he insisted upon getting lemonade for them, and the journey from the piazza to the cafe was quite long, so there was much time for chat before his return, and every moment of it was improved, while Trixy, seated on a low stool, with her head in her mother's lap, seemed slumbering as peacefully as if in her bed, and the physician at the hotel had assured Trif that the salt air at night was not in the least unwholesome, but quite the reverse.

When Harry returned, followed by a waiter with a tray, and it was learned that he had not forgotten the smallest member of the party, Trixy awoke opportunely, and felt so refreshed that she had to relieve herself of superabundant vitality by tripping to and fro on the broad walk at the edge of the beach, with several children with whom she had become acquainted. They were having a glorious time when Trixy suddenly espied Kate and Jermyn; then she lost interest in her companions and began to stare.

The objects of her attention did not notice her; they would not have been conscious of the presence of the President of the United States, had that distinguished person passed them in the full glare of the occasional lamps. They were not talking love, nor anything remotely resembling it, but they were entirely absorbed in each other, which answered the same purpose. Jermyn had promised a brother subaltern, only two or three days before, some coaching in the mysteries of ballistics, and for this very evening, but he forgot all about it, and the subaltern, who looked anxiously about for Jermyn and finally found him, saw for himself that his chances were very slight, so he sat down at the edge of the promenade and engaged Trixy in conversation. The child soon remarked:

"You don't think they're a couple of fools, do you?"

"They? Who?" asked the officer.

"Why, Lieutenant Jermyn and Miss Trewman."


"Certainly not! What an odd question! If you were a few years older, young lady, you yourself would think them eminently sensible."

"Oh, is that true? Well, I'm glad of it, 'cause a while ago Aunt Fee said if they wasn't fools they'd make a match of it. How do people make matches, anyhow? What do they make 'em of?"

"Upon my word, young woman," replied the youth, after a quiet laugh, "you're of a very inquiring turn of mind. Perhaps you had better put that question to your mother—no, not now."

"But they know, don't they? 'Cause if they don't, how are they to make one?"

"That's for themselves to find out," answered the young man, recalling an experience or two of his own which had not been successful. "By the way, how many wells have you dug to-day?"

"I don't remember," said Trixy, going into a brown study. The young officer strolled off to struggle by himself with his problem, leaving Trixy with her own. A possible aid to solution came to the child's mind. Exclaiming to herself, "Why, of course!" she began to walk, looking carefully at every person she met. Soon she saw Jermyn and Kate and attached herself to them.

"What is it, dear?" asked Kate in a tone so tender that any hesitation the child may have had vanished at once.

"Have you made it?"

"Made what?"

"Oh, if you don't know, it don't mind, I s'pose. Lieutenant Prewser thought you did know, or I wouldn't have asked you."

"What on earth is the child talking about?" asked Kate.

"Explain yourself, Trixy," said Jermyn. "What did Prewser say we knew how to do?"

"Well, come to think of it, he didn't say you knew, but he said it was for you to find out."

"But what was it?" persisted Kate.

"Why, 'twas how to make a match."

Kate suddenly averted her head, and acted as if she wanted to run away. Jermyn took her hand—gently, very gently, yet with sufficient force to detain her. Then he said:

"Trixy, your mother wants you, this very instant."

---

# CHAPTER XV.
## THE UNEXPECTED.

WHAT Jermyn and Kate said to each other in the two or three minutes immediately following Trixy's departure was entirely their own affair, and need not be repeated here; beside, they never afterward agreed exactly as to what it was. Suffice it to say that they walked somewhat rapidly in the direction of the disappearing child, and parted pleasantly. Kate joined her brother and Trif, and asked how they had secreted themselves so successfully, when she and Jermyn had been seeking them everywhere for the last half-hour. She asked also if the night was not simply superb—heavenly! and whether they weren't the stupidest people in the world to sit there quietly while the air was simply entrancing. For herself, she thought it an absolute sin to sit still in such weather, so she begged Trixy to take a little walk with her.

The child was quite willing, so the couple strolled a few moments. Soon Trixy asked:

"Does lovely nights always make you so dreadful quiet?"

"Am I quiet? I was thinking about something. There! I shall stop thinking about it. But, Trixy dear, how did you and Lieutenant Prewser come to talk about—about such things?"

"What things?"

"Don't you remember what you said to Lieutenant Jermyn and me?"

"No—o—o," drawled Trixy, whose mind had roamed over several other subjects in the past quarter hour. "What was it?"

"Oh, never mind it," said Kate hastily, "if you don't recall it."

"Oh, yes; it was about match-makin', wasn't it?"

"Yes," Kate answered, so savagely that the child started. "Did you ask your mother about it?"

"No. I was goin' to, but they all was talkin' about somethin' else, so I didn't get a chance."

"Then don't. There are some things about which little girls shouldn't talk, and about which their mammas don't like them to talk, and this is one of them; so don't mention it to your mother at all. Do you understand me?"

"Ye—es," replied Trixy, with a drawl which indicated doubt. "But mamma says, whenever I want to know anythin' about anythin' I must come and ask her right away."

"Very well, let me ask her for you, about this, won't you? You know that I love you very dearly, and wouldn't like your mamma to think badly of you in any way, so——"

"Then if you love me so much," interrupted Trixy, "why don't you give me all the dolls you said you would?"

"How shamefully forgetful I am! My dear child, you shall have those dolls to-morrow, if I have to go all the way to Norfolk for them."

"Good! good! good!"

"But," continued Kate, with an uplifted finger, which looked very impressive in the semi-darkness, "not—one—single—doll, if you say a word about this matter to your mother."

"All right!"

"You are sure you will not forget?"

"Ever so sure. If I find myself thinkin' about it at all I'll just say 'Dolls, dolls, dolls' to myself as hard as I can, and then all the think will go out of my mind."

"That's a good girl."

Then Kate lifted Trixy, embraced her, kissed her, and called her the dearest little girl on the face of the earth, after which, greatly to the child's astonishment, she hurried Trixy to her mother and excused herself, saying that she had suddenly found the night air much damper than she had supposed.

No sooner did Jermyn leave Kate's side than he went to the ball-room, the office, and about the piazzas, asking every acquaintance whether Prewser had been seen in the course of the evening. Finally he found his comrade and a reproachful face in Prewser's own quarters, and after some sharp questioning he promised to help the young man at ballistics and anything else so long as he lived. Prewser asked if congratulations were in order, and Jermyn frowned and said "Nonsense," but he afterwards whistled merrily and Prewser began to nurse some suspicions.

"Trixy, dear," said Fenie the next morning, while preparing for breakfast, "if I were you I wouldn't follow a lady and gentleman while they are promenading in the evening. It isn't ladylike. I am sure that your mamma will tell you that I am right."

Trif looked amusedly at her sister and said, "One word for others and two for yourself," but she added her own cautions to Fenie's, and said she ought to have called Trixy away from Kate and Jermyn the evening before.

"Why, I only—" began Trixy. Then she stopped and exclaimed "Dolls."

"What have dolls to do with it?" asked Fenie.

"Lots—just lots. I'm going to have 'em if I don't—oh, I nearly told."

"Told what?"

"Why, that—oh, Dolls! Dolls! Dolls! There."

"Trif," exclaimed Fenie, "I do believe the child has lost her senses."

"Oh, no I haven't, but—Dolls! Dolls! Dolls!"

"Trixy,—"

"Fenie, do be quiet," exclaimed Trif. "Trixy, run down to the table and tell our waiter we will be there very soon, so he may have the oysters ready for us. Hurry, dear."

No sooner was Trixy out of the room than Trif said:

"Fenie, you silly girl, can't you ever see anything? I suspected it last night, but now I am sure of it."

"Sure of what?"

"Why, that Kate and Jermyn are at an understanding—or sure to be. I saw when Kate rejoined us last night that something unusual had happened, and that it was not unpleasant. She acted just as I—as I felt when Phil——"

"Oh, oh, oh!" exclaimed Fenie, going quickly into some day-dreams of her own, for she and Harry were getting along capitally together. They were not engaged, but there could be no mistake as to what the dear fellow meant, and what she wanted him to mean. She did not speak another word while preparing for breakfast, for she wouldn't for worlds have told what was in her mind—not even to her sister—yet she feared she would tell it if she spoke at all. But wasn't it delightful? She would marry Harry, in the course of time, and Kate would marry Jermyn. She wondered which couple would be first at the altar. What a delightful party of friends they would be, the two couples, with Trif and Phil!

The girl's reverie was so delightful that even breakfast did not destroy it, although she had the healthy appetite to which young women have an inherent right. She took the customary morning walk along the beach with Trif and Trixy, but there was an expectant look in her eye which Trif told herself would delight Harry when he saw it. Trixy tried to talk with her, but got such vague replies that she gave up in despair and began to throw pebbles. Finally the sisters seated themselves on the piazza, and Trif began to wish she knew all that she suspected, for she longed to write her husband all about it. There was no sentimental nonsense in her mind about the handsome soldier who had once hoped for her heart and hand; but what good woman does not rejoice to see an honest admirer happily married— after she herself had married happily?

The longer she thought of it the surer she was that her intuitions were correct, so she said she must go and write a line to dear Phil. Fenie accompanied her, but when Trif reached her room Fenie was invisible, for the girl had caught a glimpse of Kate in one of the halls, and had hurried toward her. Fenie was thinking about Kate and Jermyn, so she put her arm about Kate, drew her into a parlor in which there chanced to be no one else, kissed her, and exclaimed:

"You darling girl, I'm so happy about it!"

"So am I, dear," Kate replied, returning Fenie's endearments in kind; "but I do think Harry might have said something to me, after all that I have done for him."

"Harry?" said Fenie, with a wondering look. "Doesn't he approve of the match?"

"Approve? My dear girl, how could he have made it if he hadn't thought well of it? How strangely you talk!"

"He made it? The sly rogue! He and I have chatted together for hours every day, but I didn't imagine that anything of the sort was on his mind."

"Tryphena Wardlow!" exclaimed Kate. "Will you tell me what you are talking about?"

"About you and Lieutenant Jermyn, to be sure."

"Oh, Fenie!" Kate flushed deeply before she continued: "He and I have become pleasantly acquainted, and I esteem him very highly, but can you imagine for a moment that I am anything more than the acquaintance of a gentleman whom I never saw until this week? How did you get so crazy a fancy?"

Fenie went down into the valley of humiliation, and said she was sure she didn't know, unless something that Trixy had said—no, something that Trixy hadn't said—that is, Trixy had behaved so strangely——

"I don't believe," said Kate frigidly, "that if the cases were reversed I would attach any importance to the babble of a child. In the circumstances, I think I ought to be told what Trixy did say, for she talks with every one, and I should like to know whether it is safe for me to remain here any longer. I supposed it was safe for me to be here with your sister as chaperone, but so long as she has her dreadful child with her no one's reputation is safe. I shall return home at once. Fortunately Harry's business which brought him to Norfolk is finished, so there is no reason for our remaining here any longer."

Fenie burst into tears, but Kate had her own trouble to think of, so she remained indignant. She recalled what Trixy had repeated the night before, as having been said by some officer; she herself had been too—well, too surprised and embarrassed at the moment, and too exhilarated a moment or two later, to think about the first cause of what passed between her and Jermyn, but she certainly was not going to remain where her name could give occupation to idle tongues.

"Aunt Fee," exclaimed Trixy, appearing suddenly at the door of the parlor, "I've been lookin' everywhere for you. Mamma asked me to find you for her."

"Trixy," asked Kate, "what silly things have you been saying about me?"

"Not any. Every time I was goin' to say anythin' I just said 'Dolls' instead. Didn't I, Aunt Fee?"

"Then how did your aunt know——"

"Oh, are you all here?" exclaimed Trif, entering the parlor. "I only sent for you, Fenie, to let you know that I am going to write my letter on the piazza instead of in my room; 'tis so much pleasanter out of doors. Don't you— why, my dear sister, what is the matter?"

The girl, who was thinking only of the impending departure of the young man who was all the world to her, hurried from the room, followed by Trixy. Kate began at once to complain to Trif of the child's telling—she knew not what, and that was the dreadful thing about it. When Trif learned what Kate's fears and suspicions were she said:

"Trixy has told nothing; she has had nothing to tell. If any one is to blame, it is I, who could not help imagining, and hoping too, and talking to my sister about it. If there's nothing to it I shall be dreadfully unhappy, for Jermyn is much the finest unmarried man of my acquaintance, and you are the only woman I know who is entirely worthy of him."

"Aunt Fee's cryin' awful, mamma," said Trixy, returning to the parlor.

Trif looked reproachfully at Kate, who showed signs of relenting, although she was having a severe struggle with her pride.

"When are you goin' to Norfolk to get my dolls?" asked Trixy.

Kate laughed, despite herself; Trif embraced her and whispered something which made Kate blush, look toward Trixy, and say:

"Run quickly, dear, and tell Aunt Fee that I've been real unkind, and that—for her sake, I won't return to New York until—oh, I don't know when."

---

# CHAPTER XVI.
## COWARDS BOTH.

IF human nature could be as thoroughly ashamed of its misdeeds as it sometimes is of doings entirely to its credit, the world would be much the better for it.

Kate Trewman was very sure, after her interview with Trif, Fenie and Trixy, that she had never done or said anything the night before that was not entirely womanly and honest, but the mere thought of meeting Jermyn face to face in broad daylight made her tremble as abjectly as if she were a criminal and Jermyn an officer of the law. She determined to keep her room all day; when dusk came she would go down to the piazza with Trif and Fenie, and then if Jermyn joined them, as she ardently hoped he would, he could not see in her face all that she felt her heart was putting there.

By a coincidence, not entirely odd, Jermyn was feeling very like Kate. He felt that he had acted hastily, although he could not see what else there was for a gentleman to do in the circumstances into which that dreadful Trixy had forced him. Fortunately the duties of the section-room would absorb him for some hours, but afterwards—what? It had been his custom for two years to spend an hour or two each day at the hotel, chatting with old acquaintances and forming new ones, but he could not trust himself to-day.

He recalled some romantic affairs of his earlier days, and the embarrassment of some meetings, and he persuaded himself that it was entirely for Kate's sake that he did not wish to encounter her suddenly that morning. But what could he do? Ha! He had it. He would run up to Norfolk and be measured for the new uniform which he had long been promising himself. The general commanding the department was soon to make his annual official visit to the fort; there would be an inspection and parade which should, if possible, exceed any of the weekly affairs, and if the Trewmans remained until that time, as he hoped they might, he would like to appear to the best possible advantage before the one woman in the world.

The Norfolk boat chanced to be very slow that morning, and as the weather was quite warm Jermyn made his way as far forward as possible to get the air. Most of the other passengers had done likewise, but Jermyn found a vacant chair near some brother officers and made haste to take it. Two or three minutes later he saw, seated very near him, and reading as industriously as if her book were the most interesting in the world, Kate Trewman. Kate well knew who was seated near her, but she could not help looking shyly toward him.

"What a delightful surprise!" said Jermyn, bravely, as he moved his chair toward Kate's.

"Very kind of you," Kate murmured. "I had some shopping to do, and as my brother has already made me acquainted with some of the business streets, and as I could not persuade him to accompany me, I ventured alone. The truth is, I promised Trixy Highwood some dolls before I left New York, and she reminded me of them yesterday, and I think 'tis dreadfully cruel to disappoint a child—don't you?"

"Indeed I do, when the child chances to be so interesting as Trixy." Jermyn cudgelled his wits a moment before continuing: "May I ask whether you know the ways of Norfolk shops? Some of the dealers regard Northern people as specially desirable prey, but there are others who make special concessions to us people of the fort. Won't you let me make you acquainted with some of them? After that, you may banish me when you will."

"You are very kind. Oh, Mr. Jermyn, weren't these waters the scene of that wonderful fight between the Merrimac and the Monitor?"

Jermyn immediately began the story of the historic naval engagement, and that Kate might see the localities more clearly he borrowed a glass from the pilot, and he begged permission to steady Kate's arm while she used the glass—the old boat trembled so provokingly, he said, and Kate herself admitted that she never had been on a boat whose deck was more unsteady, so Jermyn continued to assist her until nothing remained to be seen but the docks of Norfolk. Then he escorted her to two or three shops, making every possible excuse to remain with her. Finally, he said:

"Would you mind my remaining with you while you select those dolls? I used to have to buy such things, when my sisters were younger, and it would give me great pleasure to recall the sensation."

Kate could not refuse a request made in such terms, so the couple were soon having much amusement in discussing the utterly inhuman features which manufacturers succeed in imposing upon dolls. The selection consumed much time; meanwhile there came into the shop an officer's wife, newly arrived at the fort, who asked Jermyn if he might be going to the navy-yard, across the river, for she had come from an interior town where naval vessels never had been seen, and she did long to look at some, if only for a moment or two, and Jermyn said he would be delighted to escort her to and through the yard, where he knew every one, and he asked Kate whether she would not accompany them?

Kate did not say "No"; she was by that time in a frame of mind which would have made her equal to tramping through mud for the sake of having Jermyn beside her. While at the yard, she noted with delight the heartiness with which all the naval officers greeted Jermyn. Trif had whispered to her, only a few hours before, that she herself had once been almost in love with Jermyn, and that she still believed no other bachelor alive was his equal, but Kate had been a woman long enough to attach more importance to men's opinions of men than to women's. Luncheon was served for the party on one of the war vessels, and each lady was toasted, and Kate noted that when her own name was given, Jermyn drained his glass with a look at her which made her feel uncomfortable yet happy.

The party returned to Old Point by a boat which did not reach the pier until after dark, and as the officer's wife had never before been in Norfolk alone her husband was at the pier, in much anxiety, to look for her, and escort her home, and the pier was so covered with freight that Jermyn thought it his duty to insist that Kate should take his arm, which he held very closely to his side without any remonstrance from the owner, and then he insisted upon finding her brother or Trif before he left her.

"'Tis all right," whispered Trif to Fenie, as she saw them approaching.

"About the dolls?" asked Trixy, anxiously. "Do you think them's in the bundle that he's carryin'?"

"No, you silly child!" said Fenie. "Your mother means———"

Fenie received a warning pinch, but it was too late, for the child exclaimed: "Oh, I know!" and made a sudden dash in the direction of the approaching couple. Trif snatched at Trixy's dress; there was a ripping, tearing sound, and away went the child, while behind her floated something like a train.

"Oh, I'm so glad!" she exclaimed, stopping before Jermyn and Kate so suddenly as to separate them.

"Yes," said Kate. "Here are the dolls, dear."

"I'm awful glad to get 'em; my, what a big bundle! But that wasn't what I meant."

"What else?" asked Kate, in entire innocence.

"Why, that you're bein' nice to Mr. Jermyn. Mamma and Aunt Fee have been talkin' about you all day, and hopin' you wouldn't be a fool—that's what they said; I never say such things about a lady—no indeed! Say, you're engaged, aren't you? 'Cause———"

"Take the package to your mother, Trixy, and let her open it for you," said Jermyn quickly. "Miss Trewman, please don't hurry away; do take my arm again, just for a moment; thank you. I merely wished to say—shall we walk a moment?—to say that our friends seem to take unusual interest in us; interest of a kind which I'm sure neither of us has said a word to justify."

"Not a word, I'm sure," assented Kate.

"But I can't endure," continued Jermyn rapidly, "to risk, merely through the prattle of a child, the most delightful friendship I ever made. Last night I said to you—but why repeat it? I've no right to expect you to endure any annoyance, for my sake, but if you chance to like me as much as last night you let me think you do, can't we afford to make light of such chatter as that provoking child may inflict upon us? Good men are plentiful—better men than I; but to me there is only one woman in all the world, and I can't bear the thought of giving up hope of her until she herself commands me. I assure you that I am entirely in earnest."

"I couldn't suspect you of flirting," said Kate, softly.

"Thank you," said Jermyn, pressing closely to his side the little hand which was trembling on his arm. "I won't ask you for any promises, except that you will allow yourself to become well acquainted with me. You are with friends who love you dearly, and one of them knows me of old. There can be nothing to cause embarrassment between us, except——"

"Except Trixy?" interrupted Kate, with a silvery laugh.

"Bless you for laughing about it!" said Jermyn, earnestly. "If you can continue to do so, then——"

"One can get accustomed to almost anything," said Kate, with another laugh, although why she laughed she was sure she did not know.

"If 'can' could mean 'will,' and if I could be 'anything'—" said Jermyn. He did not complete the sentence, so Kate looked shyly up at him. They had walked so far that they were beyond the lights of the hotel, but the girl could see that her companion's face, always strong and earnest, seemed intently fixed upon something far ahead. They had walked all the way to the little lighthouse, and just beyond it, and there are few darker places than the base of a lighthouse. The darkness gave Kate courage, so she whispered:

"It shall mean 'will,' if you wish it so."

"Heaven bless you!" Then—what strange influences there are in darkness!—Jermyn threw his arms about Kate and kissed her.

Some student of love has said that kisses gain force by delay. Jermyn's was the first kiss Kate Trewman had ever received from a man who professed to love her, so between astonishment and many other things which she did not understand and could not have called up and thought about at the time had her life depended upon it, she did not resist the kiss nor the several that followed it.

"My angel!" said Jermyn. "You will be my wife?"

"How can I help it?" asked Kate, softly, "after—after what has happened?"

"Hurrah!" sounded a child's voice behind them.

"Trixy!"

"I didn't mean to do nothin'," the child explained. "I was just walkin' along behind you, 'cause you both looked so splendid, and walked so nice together, but when you kissed each other——"

"Trixy!" exclaimed Kate, "I did nothing of the sort!"

"Didn't you? Then I don't think you was very polite."

# CHAPTER XVII.
## THE COURAGE OF JOY.

SOME of the least explicable changes of manner are the most genuine, so it is not necessary to assign any reason for the fact that on the way back to the hotel Jermyn and Kate, who had both been under considerable restraint a few moments before, talked as freely and rapidly as if they had been acquainted for years. The only indication that there was more than one thought between them was the care with which they kept Trixy in sight and reach, so that her little tongue could not wag until it had been put under proper curb by Trixy's mother. On the other hand, they kept her far enough from them for her not to overhear anything that they were saying to each other, and their frequent recalls, whenever the child attempted to skip or run, had the effect of soon making Trixy appear as if she were a prisoner under close guard.

Even when the hotel was reached the child was kept within view yet out of hearing, while Jermyn and Kate sat down with Trif. Fortunately for them, Harry and Fenie just then thought of some one whom they wanted to find in the ball-room, and they were glad of some one who would keep Trif from being alone.

Jermyn began with military directness by saying:

"Miss Trewman, may I ask one of my oldest friends to congratulate me?"

"Yes," Kate replied, "if you will let her include me in the congratulations."

"Oh, you dear people!" exclaimed Trif. "There's nothing that I would rather have heard."

"You don't think it shockingly sudden?" asked Kate.

"Not I—considering what either of you might have missed by delay."

"I assure you," said Kate, "that not a word would have been said about it for months—it all came so suddenly—if it hadn't been for Trixy."

"Where is that child?" asked Jermyn, rising in alarm and looking in every direction.

"She's looking at her dolls," Trif replied. "No, she isn't. Dear me! I arranged those dolls for her on a chair not ten minutes ago."

"Not ten minutes ago?" asked Jermyn dreamily.

"It seems ten hours ago—ten days," whispered Kate dreamily.

"My dear children," said Trif, although Kate was only three years younger than she and Jermyn was older by several years, "you ought to be the happiest people alive, except Phil and I; but to keep the matter to ourselves for a while, if only to divert attention and prevent impertinent curiosity while Kate is down here—you know how some of the best of people will talk—don't tell any one—although I'm sure that I must tell Fenie, who can't help telling Harry, but no one else need know."

"But, my dear madam," said Jermyn, once more rising and peering earnestly in every direction, "your interesting daughter already knows. I do wish I knew where to look for her."

"Trixy knows? How on earth did she learn?"

"Tell her—if you can," said Kate to Jermyn.

"I am sure that you would do it more gracefully," said Jermyn.

"Oh," began Kate, "we were walking along the beach, talking about—never mind what. I hadn't the faintest idea how far we were from the hotel, and the first thing I knew we were near the lighthouse, and I didn't know that any one else was anywhere near us—indeed, I didn't think. Just then Mr. Jermyn—oh, the artfulness of some men—Mr. Jermyn—he———"

"He suddenly recognized Miss Trewman as his superior officer for all time, and he made the salute which custom has sanctioned for such occasions," interrupted Jermyn.

"Very gracefully done," murmured Kate with a tender look.

"What?—the salute? Your remark encourages me to———"

"No, you horrid fellow; the explanation."

"But what has this to do with Trixy?" asked Trif.

"Only this; it seems that she had been following us all the while, and she heard it."

Trif pursed her lips a moment, and laughed before she said:

"I suppose that soldiers are so accustomed to noisy salutes that they don't always think———"

"Oh," said Kate, "I'm sure she didn't hear the kiss, because I didn't, and I think—oh, Trif, you're too mean for anything! To make me———"

"I think I made some remarks afterward," said Jermyn, "but they were interrupted by a shout of 'Hurrah,' and on looking around we saw Trixy."

"She shan't trouble you again!" exclaimed Trif. "I'll take her home—to-morrow."

"Please don't!" exclaimed Kate.

"How could you be so cruel?" asked Jermyn.

"You inconsistent, incomprehensible couple. A moment ago you were complaining that——"

"But haven't you any mercy for Harry and Fenie?" asked Kate. "They are so ecstatically happy here."

"Quite right, my dear!" said Jermyn gravely. "Harry and Fenie, to be sure!"

"But they can see each other in New York quite as well as if they were here," argued Trif.

"But what is to become of me?" asked Kate. "If you go home, Fenie will go with you, and Harry will want to hurry after, and I can't remain here alone, and you are the only married woman of my acquaintance who is here, and who knows."

"My dear girl!" exclaimed Trif. "I beg a thousand pardons. Let me see; what can I do? I don't see what, except to caution Trixy very carefully; and as she is the most conscientious little thing in the world, and——"

"And the leakiest," added Kate.

"Be quiet, Kate! I won't have the dear child maligned. She never tells anything she is ordered not to—unless she is asked. I shall tell her that she will make great unhappiness for two people who love her dearly if she says anything to anybody about anything which she has heard or—ahem!—seen this evening. Of course, no one will question her, for no one has any reason to suspect anything, and, of course, nothing in the manner of either of you will give any ground for curiosity."

"'Twould be awful—simply too awful," moaned Kate, "if anyone should learn what has happened on so short acquaintance. Beside, I'd be the principal sufferer, whereas it wasn't in the least particular my fault."

"'Twas all your fault, my dear," protested Jermyn. "If you hadn't been the most incomparable woman in all the world——"

"Please don't forget," interrupted Kate, "that we are not alone."

"I'll take Trixy aside at once," said Trif, "and caution her thoroughly."

"You will make us everlastingly your debtors," said Jermyn. "Let me find her for you."

While the young man was absent, the two women talked as rapidly and earnestly and ecstatically as only women can talk about the most important event—but one—that can befall one of their sex. Almost as soon as Jermyn returned with the child, an orderly from the fort appeared with the word that the officer was wanted at his company quarters, so Jermyn bade a reluctant adieu, and hurried away.

As he passed through the postern gate of the fort, he met an officer who seemed to be looking for some one, and who exclaimed:

"Hurry along, old fellow! Every one is waiting impatiently."

"Every one waiting? What has happened?"

"You'll learn in a moment."

"Has some high government official died, and are all the troops at the fort to attend the funeral?"

"No such bad luck; at any rate, you won't have to go into mourning." So saying, the officer led Jermyn into the club, where the wondering man found several officers of his own rank, and all bachelors. As Jermyn entered, all arose, with glasses in their hands, and one of them shouted:

"Here's Jermyn!"

"Jermyn!" shouted the others in chorus, after which each man drained his glass and refilled it. Then some one shouted:

"Hats, off gentlemen! Here's 'Her!'"

"Her!" responded the chorus, and again the glasses were drained.

"What are you fellows talking about?" asked Jermyn, with a savage frown.

"Don't lose your temper, old fellow," said one of the party. "You know that we're not given to prying into the personal affairs of our comrades, but this information came to us unsought."

"Not only unsought," said Lieutenant Prewser, "but we did all in our power to avoid getting it—didn't we, Groston?"

"Indeed we did. We tried to change the subject of conversation, or, more properly speaking, of report, but she wouldn't have it. She got back to it every time, and she stuck to it until she had her say."

"She? Who?"

"Trixy."

"Heavens!" muttered Jermyn, while his face became very red.

"The accused displays the customary sign of guilt," remarked the oldest officer of the party.

"Really, Jermyn," said Prewser, "I never met anyone who was more determined to talk. If I'd been alone I wouldn't have said anything about it, but as there were three of us, and we all tried to dissuade her, and she persisted in offering circumstantial evidence—ahem!—too strong to be set aside, we thought it only fair that we, who have fought and bled and died with you, or expect to do so, should be the first to congratulate you. To think of all the women who've angled for you, yet whom you've escaped! And you've made such a glorious capture, too! If we hadn't agreed that there should be only two toasts on this happy occasion, I should be in favor of our drinking also to Trixy."

"Confound her!" exclaimed Jermyn, thinking only of Kate's feelings should Trixy have talked further before he captured her and led her to her mother, "are you fellows so foolish as to attach any importance to what a child like that may say?"

"Does the accused desire that the evidence shall be reviewed, item by item, in his presence?" asked some one. "Only three of us have heard it, but if the accused himself insists——"

"Be quiet!" Jermyn roared.

"Your secret is safe with us, old fellow," said Prewser, "as you know well, so forgive us if we've been a little effusive in our rejoicing for your sake. Go to your quarters and to happy dreams. Jove! how I envy you!"

"So—so say we all of us," repeated the others in unison, as Jermyn beat a hasty retreat.

The miseries which Jermyn wished Trixy during the short walk from the club to his quarters quite out-Heroded Herod. Once fairly by himself, however, his joy banished his anger. Let the boys laugh among themselves! They all envied him, didn't they say so? How could he ever sleep, after so exciting an evening? What had he ever done that he should be so richly blessed as he would be with Kate Trewman for his wife?

There must have been a special Providence watching over him in other days when he thought himself in love, even when he failed to win Tryphosa Wardlow, and, within a few days—how long passed they seemed!—when he could not keep the face of Trif's pretty sister out of his mind, and wouldn't have done so if he could!

But how very long the coming night would be! He had known long nights while on picket, when his battery was on duty in the Indian country and he had looked forward to them with dread, but now there would be twelve hours, at the very least, before he could again gaze upon the face of the woman who was all the world to him. What could he do to pass the time? Study?—bosh! Read? No; he must sleep, for he owed it to Kate to appear his very best the next day. Still, it was only ten o'clock; he never retired before eleven. He would read a little while; read some poetry—something he had done but little in late years.

He had read but a few minutes when there was a knock at the door and a servant handed him a letter addressed in writing which he did not recognize. He opened it and read:

We return to New York by the morning train. You had scarcely left us when two ladies whom I've known only two or three days came to tell me how glad they were of the news. When I learned what they meant I expressed surprise, but they said that every one in the hotel knew of it—some one had overheard Trixy talking of it to two or three officers. That child!

Sorrowfully,

KATE.

# CHAPTER XVIII
## THE WOOING O' IT.

THERE was a lot of misery—four rooms full of it—when Kate Trewman announced to the Highwood party and her brother that she could never, never, never again face the gossips and the other people at the hotel after the story of her engagement had got about with the infinity of detail which Trixy had imparted and the additions which are inevitable when a story is passed from lip to lip. Trif had promised to go sailing the very next day with some new friends, Fenie had promised several dances for the "Ladies' Night" at the fort, which would be the next night but one, and Harry and Fenie had agreed to make a little trip which Harry thought would be peculiarly delightful, and Fenie agreed with him, although she did not know why.

But Kate was obdurate. She admitted to Trif that she loved Jermyn dearly, strange though it might seem, but for that very reason her self-respect was stronger than ever, and although she could endure anything for her own sake she was not willing that anything should occur, or that anything which had occurred, should make the dear fellow laughed at and talked about. People were so mean! Who knew but some one would say that she had tried to catch him, and succeeded? The idea!

"But Kate," argued Trif, "there's no need of your being seen if you'll consent to remain a day or two longer. You've only to remain in your room while I make my sailing trip with my friends, and Harry and Fenie have their little outing. You won't be alone; think of the delightful thoughts that will keep you company! The day after my trip I'll make a special luncheon in my room, in honor of the happy couple, and it will be entirely right, as your brother will bring Jermyn. You certainly couldn't be so heartless as to depart without seeing him once more, and without letting him see you."

"Do you think it would be heartless—do you think it would seem so to him?"

"It certainly would, to him or to any other good man, under the circumstances," Trif replied, with extreme New England positiveness.

"Then I will remain," said Kate; upon which Trif kissed her and called her a dear good girl, and Fenie kissed her and called her a sensible girl, and Harry kissed her and said she was a good sister, and Trixy offered to kiss her but was rudely pushed away.

Jermyn knew nothing of this conversation. He had done much desperate thinking after receiving Kate's note, and one consequence was that he looked across the parade ground, saw that lights were still burning in the adjutant's office and the home of the post commandant, so he hurried over to the adjutant and made an application for leave of absence for a week, on important personal business. The post adjutant looked astonished, for leaves of absence in the army are charged against the month's leave which each officer is allowed once a year in time of peace, and the adjutant knew well that Jermyn had been carefully "saving his time" for a month's run to the Pacific Coast during the coming summer. Still, Jermyn pleaded urgency, and begged for an immediate decision; and the post commandant, who was a large-hearted gentleman, and also a close observer of the individual members of his command, granted the leave; so the next morning, very early, before any one at the hotel was stirring, Jermyn invaded a lighthouse boat which he knew was to go to Norfolk very early. His plan was to get upon the steamer which started from Norfolk for the train, miles away, touching at Old Point *en route.* Neither Kate nor her brother should know of his proximity until the train started; after that,—well, Kate could not be other than the woman he thought her, so she would be glad to see him, and her brother, beside being a gentleman, was himself in love; so he would certainly give the couple some opportunities for conversation during the trip to New York.

While this was going on, the Admiral, who had been somewhat upset by his exciting experience of two or three preceding days, and had been restoring himself by a veteran seaman's favorite remedy, rest, got out of his room very early, and sauntered about the beach in search of a proper appetite for breakfast. It did not help him much to meet Jermyn and hear the young man's story of disappointment, yet he heartily approved of the fellow's spirit and wished him the happy time which undoubtedly would be his. The excitement caused by the interview gave the old gentleman the appetite for which he longed, so he went in at once to breakfast, at which he lingered long.

As he sat at table, the train-boat from Norfolk came in, and the Admiral looked through the window toward the pier, hoping for a glimpse of Kate. Evidently she had escaped him, for she was not with any of the parties which moved down from the hotel; probably she was already in the crowd, which always is an hour in advance of starting time, and he did not like to bid a lady good-bye when there were all sorts of people around to hear what was said.

As the boat cast off and started for Cape Charles, the southern terminus of the railway, the old gentleman raised his coffee-cup to his lips, and murmured:

"God bless them!"

"Who's you a-blessin'?" asked Trixy, who had entered the breakfast-room and had been moving by circuitous lines to "s'prise" the Admiral.

"Why, Trixy! Good morning! I've not seen you for several days. Do sit down and take some breakfast with me. Tell me some news."

"There ain't no news," said Trixy. "Yes there is too; but mamma says I mustn't ever tell any more news until I'm a big woman. And I can't take breakfast just now, 'cause I just was sent down to ask the waiter to send Miss Trewman's breakfast up to her room, 'specially a cup of coffee."

"Miss Trewman's breakfast? Why—Miss Trewman has gone to New York."

"Oh, no, she hasn't. She changed her mind. Mamma made her do it."

"Trixy, do you mean to say," asked the Admiral, as he arose hastily from the table, "that Miss Trewman isn't on the boat which started for the train at Cape Charles?"

"I mean to say she's up in her room," Trixy replied, "for I just came from there and I saw her. She said she wanted that coffee awfully, too, so I mustn't wait any longer to see the waiter; but I'll come back in a minute and take some breakfast with you, if you like."

"Ah—er," stammered the Admiral, who had been thinking rapidly and looking at the lighthouse tug, which was already steaming back from Norfolk, "suppose we hold the engagement over until to-morrow morning? The truth is, I've practically finished my own breakfast, so I wouldn't be proper company. Besides, I've just thought of something which ought to be attended to this instant."

"All right," said Trixy. "I'm goin' to have one comp'ny meal to-day anyway, cause mamma's goin' to give a splendid little dinner in her room to Miss Trewman and Mr. Jermyn."

"Indeed! Excuse me, my dear, but I must hurry."

The Admiral hurried out of the room, and, despite his years and his dignity, ran toward "The Hole," a sheltered portion of the harbor where small craft usually anchored. He got as near as possible to the lighthouse tug, and waved his handkerchief violently. Just as the anchor of the tug dropped, a sailor reported to the officer in charge:

"Signal from the shore, sir!"

"Don't notice it," was the reply, made gruffly. "Hang the impertinence of some of these spring visitors."

"Yes, sir. I think it's Admiral Allison a-signallin', sir."

"Ah, that's different! Lower away! I'll go ashore for him."

The tug's boat had scarcely touched the beach when the Admiral gave the prow a mighty shove and shouted, "Shove off! Give way!" first wetting his feet thoroughly. Then he sprang like a cat from thwart to thwart until he got aft and dropped beside the astonished officer, whispering:

"Charley, you were at the Naval Academy while I was on duty there!"

"Yes, Admiral, and you were the best friend I ever had there. I couldn't have pulled through if it hadn't been for you, as you well know!"

"I'm glad you think so, my dear boy, for I want some special help from you to-day. Up anchor, and let me catch that train for New York."

"Why, Admiral, you know what a slow old tub this is, and we've been blowing off steam."

"Never mind. Help me to catch that train. Burn out a boiler, if necessary, and charge it to me. I'll stand a court-martial rather than lose that train."

Within five minutes the tug was rounding the pier in front of the hotel and the Admiral was compounding a prescription which is highly esteemed at sea by elderly gentlemen who are suffering from great excitement and wet feet. Black smoke poured so densely from the boat's single funnel that a naval officer who was enjoying a brief outing at the hotel and had got out of bed early to enjoy as much as possible of it, told his wife that probably a buoy had strayed from its moorings somewhere and some sea-captain had been complaining by telegraph to the authorities at Washington.

The chase was a hard one; the train-boat had fully ten minutes the start of the tug, but the Admiral, who stood forward ready to hurry ashore, remarked that it usually took fully ten minutes to get all the passengers, luggage and freight from the boat to the train. When finally he went over the side he said:

"Charley, keep your eye on the rear platform. If I wave my handkerchief you'll know I'm safely aboard. Then wait as long as the train does; if it starts at once, steam along up the bay until you see it stop. I'll get the conductor to pull up and let us off."

"Us?"

"Yes; Jermyn and me."

It was none of the young officer's business, as he told himself, but he could not help wondering what was up between the Admiral and Jermyn. He saw the old gentleman scramble upon the rear platform of the last car, and at that very instant the train started, so the tug's nose was put up Chesapeake Bay, while her commander told himself that the chasing of a big ferry boat by a small tug was a sort of service for which boats of the lighthouse service were not designed, and that the next time the Admiral wanted anything of the sort done, and wanted a locomotive chased afterward, he hoped there would be a torpedo boat in the harbor.

Meanwhile the Admiral was making his way through the train in search of Jermyn, while the latter, moving from front to rear, was looking for Kate. The two men met suddenly in the vestibule between two cars.

"Admiral!" exclaimed Jermyn. "Are you too going to New York?"

"Not this time, dear boy. Neither are you. She's changed her mind—Miss Trewman—she's still at the hotel. Where's the conductor? Hang it, Charley will never be able to catch us if we go on at this rate. Where's the bell-rope?"

The old gentleman, who was quite short, sprang lightly upward, blew two long blasts, and the train began to slow. The Admiral opened the vestibule door and said:

"Come on! We'll have to jump."

Jump they did, and into some Eastern Shore mud which did not harmonize with the attire of either gentleman. As they floundered out of it, screened from the train by some scrubby bushes, the tug, which had heard the locomotive's stopping signal, blew three long blasts of her own whistle. Long before she steamed abreast of the part of the beach which the runaways had reached, the Admiral was waving his handkerchief so wildly that Jermyn insisted upon relieving him to spare him the pangs of a stiff shoulder and the danger of apoplexy.

---

# CHAPTER XIX.
## THE MISSING GUEST.

AS Trif was a prudent wife and housekeeper, she had been moaning to herself for days about the expense of the Southern trip. Nevertheless, she arranged for a lunch party regardless of expense, as befitted an occasion when two happy couples, newly made so, were to be her guests. She promised herself that she would pay for it by not buying a single new article of clothing, not even a new frock, for the coming season. She would economize in any and every way; she would let her house, furnished, for a few months, and take Trixy and Fenie and herself to some out-of-the-way place where everything was cheap, and the other boarders would not know her old clothes from the newest. Further, as she would have to send home for more money, she sat down and wrote an ecstatic confession to her husband, telling him that she really thought it her duty, as a member of society, to complete the matches which were as good as made between Harry and Fenie, Kate and Jermyn.

Then she sent to Jermyn such a note as only a great-hearted, good-hearted woman could write, after which she insisted on helping to array Kate as a queen should be dressed for her formal coronation. She was as earnest as she was sentimental, so she talked so strongly as well as romantically to Kate that the latter grew sweeter and handsomer every moment, until finally she felt as if the occasion would be one of consecration instead of a mere meeting with the man who already seemed a very old acquaintance.

Trif told her she looked like a goddess, a sacrifice, an angel, a queen—everything a good woman could be while trying to devote her love and life to a worthy man. Trif had been telling her, and Kate was in a condition of mind to believe it, that marriages were made in heaven, and despite all future ceremonies that might be necessary her obligations were already recorded above, and Kate rose to the dignity of the occasion, and looked sweeter and felt happier, although more humble and earnest than in all her life before, for were not all who were to be present quite near to her?—her brother, who seemed in the seventh heaven of happiness; Fenie, who appeared almost too beautiful, in her happiness and devotion, to be merely human; Trif, the woman who had known love for years and rejoiced in it with a nobility surpassing that of any other woman Kate had ever met; and Trixy—oh, Kate could take even Trixy to her heart. Mischief-making though the child had been, Trixy's hands and no others should strew flowers when the day came for Kate and Jermyn to be made husband and wife. What a heaven on earth this much-abused old world was, to be sure!

"Oh, Kate," exclaimed Trif, reappearing for about the twentieth time, "what do you suppose it can mean? Before breakfast I wrote Jermyn, asking him to lunch with us at noon, and I've just received word that he is not at the fort. He has gone away—gone to New York."

Kate almost tottered, so Trif hurried to support her. Suddenly Kate changed her manner and exclaimed:

"What a grand fellow he is!"

"What do you mean?" asked Trif, almost doubting her own senses. Kate looked proud, then pensive, after which she said softly:

"Last night I sent him word of what had happened—the remarks of those inquisitive women, you know, who got hold of what Trixy had said, and I told him it would be necessary for me to return—that I would go to New York this morning. He has started at once to follow me. I might have imagined, in advance, that he would do exactly that. The splendid fellow!"

"The unhappy fellow, I should say," wailed Trif. "There he goes, probably on the very train he supposed you would take, and he is looking for you, and his heart is aching as if——"

"Oh!" gasped Kate, with the manner of a tragedy queen. "I never, never thought of that."

"De lunch is served, ladies," said the colored waiter who had been busying himself in the room for some moments.

"Come along, dear," said Trif. "If you love him as I loved Phil the day after he proposed you'll have him in your heart very safely, no matter how far away he may be. The more trouble you think him in, the dearer you will love him. As to the rest of us, we will promise to talk of him only."

"Indeed, yes," added Fenie, who had heard the unwelcome news, and hastened to offer consolation. "I won't say a word about any one else—even about Harry."

"Neither will I," volunteered Trixy, who had followed her aunt into the room. "He——"

"You little——" interrupted Kate, moving toward the child with vengeful gesture, but Trixy continued:

"He looked so splendid last night when he kissed you that I haven't thought of anythin' since except the way papa kisses mamma."

Then both women blushed, and Fenie looked so oddly at Harry that the young man blushed too, but recovered sufficiently to ask Fenie whether they shouldn't set the others a good example by leading the way to the table.

Although very little time elapsed before the remainder of the party followed them, Fenie was found with brilliant roses in her cheeks, while upon her finger was a ring which none of the party but Harry had ever seen before, and Harry was looking as proud as a king, and Fenie was regarding him as if she were his most adoring and obedient subject.

"If my loss," said Kate gayly, after several significant glances from Trif had compelled her to see the brilliant upon Fenie's hand, "has been to the gain of any one else, or even to two other people, I shall endeavor to endure it bravely. I've always been sacrificing myself for my brother; I shall be glad if my long vigil is to end."

So the party became quite happy despite the missing guest, and there was so much of the merry joking that brothers and sisters can exchange that Fenie and Harry soon began to talk as if they had been engaged for months instead of moments. And how Trif, the happy wife, and Kate, the proud betrothed, did enjoy the spectacle! Kate, indeed, soon began to hold herself to account for forgetting absolutely, for at least half an hour, the loyal soul that was vainly following her and might not be able to find her until—when? She became very pensive and thoughtful; Harry must find out for her, at the fort, if possible, how to communicate with Jermyn. She would remain at the hotel, be stared at, talked about, anything, if only that the man who loved her should not remain unhappy a single moment longer than was absolutely necessary. She thought so seriously that Trixy finally remarked:

"Mamma, dear, I don't believe Miss Trewman likes this kind of lobster."

"Card for you, ma'am," said the waiter suddenly to Trif.

Trif took the card and read aloud:

"Admiral Allison; 'just for a moment.' How odd! Perhaps, Kate, 'tis something about Jermyn. You may say I'll be down in a moment."

"He's right outside de do', ma'am," the waiter replied.

"The business-like way of some men!" exclaimed Trif. "Still, it must be something important. By the way, girls, the Admiral is a delightful gentleman, and he knows the two secrets that are in our hearts to-day, and we have a vacant place at the table—show him in, waiter."

The party arose. The Admiral entered the room, and behind him came——

"Jermyn!" shouted Kate. How ridiculously thin armor is when there is a healthy heart under it! Kate rushed at Jermyn, threw her arms about him, and kissed him as affectionately as if he were a long-lost relation.

"How did you come to be here?" she finally asked.

"The Admiral brought me," Jermyn replied.

Then, shocking, yet truthful to relate, Kate kissed the Admiral also. She was the taller of the two, so she had to lean over him, but no one laughed or seemed astonished—no one but Trixy, who exclaimed, "My!" but no notice was taken of it.

"Ladies and gentleman," said the Admiral, gravely, after the excitement had subsided a little, and he stood with a lapel of his coat drawn back while he drew from his pocket a medal which hung from a clasp, "I thought when this medal was presented to me by my country that I had gained the highest honor of which an American was capable, but I am now compelled to change my opinion. Miss Trewman, the goddess of liberty will hereafter owe you a grudge."

"But, Admiral," said Kate, all blushes and brilliancy, "how could you know that he had gone, and that—that—oh, that I wanted him back?"

"Oh, I chanced to meet him, very early this morning, learned that he was going, and the reason of his sudden departure."

"And you prevented him?"

"How could I? He said that you had gone unexpectedly, and that he thought it his duty to follow you. I should have felt as he did, in similar circumstances, so I bade him God-speed."

"But he started. I don't——"

"I did, my dear," said Jermyn, "but the Admiral, with a special boat, chased our craft and the train, found me, stopped the train, and brought me back, and—here I am."

"Oh, you are, indeed! Admiral, you're an angel."

The Admiral bowed profoundly and said:

"I cannot contradict a lady."

"But how did you know—Oh, do explain what I'm sure none of us yet understand."

"The Spaniards have a saying," the old gentleman replied, "that fortunes, like miseries always travel in couples. While I was breakfasting this morning, and feeling an almost impertinent interest, I must confess, in the affairs of an estimable couple who seemed to have encountered contrary winds, Trixy——"

"Trixy?"

"Really, Miss Trewman," said Trixy, with a troubled yet appealing face, "I didn't tell him anything awful. He said you'd gone to New York, and I said he was mistaken, 'cause mamma had made you change your mind, and that mamma was goin' to give a luncheon party this mornin' to you and Mr. Jermyn, and—and—that was all I said—wasn't it, Admiral?"

"Absolutely all. Whatever has happened since has been entirely through what Trixy said."

Then Kate kissed Trixy, and told her that she was the dearest little thing that ever was born, and the information seemed to do the child a lot of good. Afterward it occurred to Kate that the man who had been the principal subject of her thoughts during the day was getting very little of her attention, and as the Admiral insisted upon departing, and Harry and Fenie had eyes only for each other, and Trif seemed entirely happy with no one to talk to, the meal passed delightfully although slowly to its close. When general conversation chanced again to begin, Fenie remarked:

"It does seem that none of us can have any more misunderstandings. There never would have been any but for Trixy, but she certainly can do no harm in the future."

"Trixy certainly has learned her lesson," said Trif.

"Papa says that some folks never get through with their lessons till they die," observed Trixy, while all the rest looked serious.

## CHAPTER XX.
### A BLISSFUL WEEK.

THE Highwoods and Trewmans started for New York a few hours after the lunch-party ended, and Jermyn accompanied them. He had wanted to do so, from the first, but found many difficulties in the way of saying so; for when women are intent upon a journey they find so much to do and talk about that a man, no matter how dear he may be to any member of the party, learns to his mortification that there are times when man is utterly uninteresting to woman.

Jermyn finally found himself so manifestly in the way that he begged Trixy, whose dolls were packed within ten minutes of the first announcement of the impending departure, to go upon the verandah with him and take a long look seaward. A friend of his had been promising to sail a yacht down from New York, and the verandah was as good as any place in the fort from which to view the offing. Besides, the Lieutenant did not care to be seen again at his quarters. He feared that a secret which several of his comrades shared with him might not be as safe as it should be, and he was in no humor to be joked about the most serious interest of his life.

In the angle of the verandah they sat, Jermyn and Trixy, the child looking seaward through her mother's opera-glass, and the officer looking into the sky, his thoughts that afternoon having a somewhat heavenly tinge.

"Oh, I believe there's the yacht—way out there! Don't you see it?"

"Where? What?" asked Jermyn, dreamily.

"Why, the yacht, of course. Don't you see that great big boat with lots of sails! That's the way yachts are, ain't it?"

"I suppose so."

"You don't look as I feel when folks is comin' to see me; though, to be sure, they don't come in yachts."

"I beg your pardon, Trixy. I fear I was thinking about something else."

"Say!" remarked Trixy, suddenly dropping the glass. "Do you know what I wish? I wish you was goin' to New York with us."

"Trixy," said Jermyn earnestly, "so do I."

"Well, why don't you?"

"Hem! I suppose it is because I haven't been asked."

"That's a funny reason! I thought big men could do anything they wanted to, without anybody tellin' 'em they could or they couldn't. When I get to be a big woman, mamma says I won't have to ask her what I can do before I do it. Won't that be lovely?"

Jermyn did not reply, so the child began again to scan the offing with the glass. Then she wanted to do something else, and Jermyn was reminded amusingly of some ways of his sisters, when those estimable women were very young.

"Say," remarked Trixy, suddenly, "mamma says you great big soldiers are just like little children in one way. You never can go any place without askin' somebody to let you."

"Your mamma is entirely right about it," said Jermyn, with a laugh.

"How funny!" said Trixy, as if talking to herself.

The child finally disappeared, but Jermyn remained. He wondered how he could explain his reappearance at the fort, after taking a week's leave only twenty-four hours before, should any awkwardness on the part of any one prevent him joining the party. He wished he might see Trif alone for a moment or two, but he knew better than to disturb a woman absorbed in the duties of packing. He was uncomfortable; he felt that he was in the way, but he pulled himself together by saying that he might as well be a thousand miles away from Trif and Kate as he was at that moment, while they were occupied as they were. He could still make a pretense of looking for that yacht, for Trixy had left the glasses in her chair. Perhaps, after their work was done, one or other of the ladies might accidentally find him, and something might be said that would give him the opportunity for which he longed.

"Mamma," said Trixy, entering the room and stumbling over trunks, "why don't Mr. Jermyn go to New York with us?"

"Oh, I do wish he could!" exclaimed Trif. "Fenie, wouldn't it be be delightful?"

"Indeed, yes," the girl replied, "but don't say anything about it to Kate, for the mention of it, when it can't be done, would simply break her heart."

Trixy propounded some more questions, but was told that her mother was very busy, and must not be bothered, so the child started in search of other company, and when she reached the beach she found the Admiral, whom she asked:

"Who is it that officers like Mr. Jermyn have to ask when they want to do somethin'?"

"Oh," said the Admiral, who was discussing the naval topic of the day with a brother officer, "why, the commandant of the fort!"

Trixy hung upon the Admiral's chair a moment or two, but what she heard was as bad as Greek to her, so she strayed away, and asked questions of other acquaintances, and she was gone so long that her mother wondered what had become of her.

When the packing was finished, to the very last article which had been overlooked, and for which the trunks had to be reopened, Kate and Fenie sat down to rest, and naturally each began to talk of the subject which was uppermost in the minds of both, and finally they became so confidential that Fenie exclaimed:

"Wouldn't it be lovely if Jermyn were going North with us?"

"Oh, Fenie!" murmured Kate, looking as Mother Eve probably looked when the gates of Eden closed behind her.

"Why don't you make him?" asked the younger woman.

"Make him? He is an officer of the Government, and has his duties to perform. Do you suppose I would dare ask him to neglect them?"

"I'm sure I can't see what duties there can be to embarrass him, for there isn't any war going on."

"No, but there seems to be so much else. Don't you remember that mysterious mission that took him and the Admiral North a few days ago? Jermyn must be of great importance, despite his modest rank, or he never would have been associated with an admiral, on public business."

"I'd ask him, any way, if he were my lover, if only to make him happy for a moment," said Fenie.

"Would you?" asked Kate. Should she be outdone in affectionate impulse by a mere girl like Fenie? She wondered what had become of Jermyn; then she said so.

"He's out at the angle of this verandah, or was a half hour ago, Trixy told me; he was looking for the yacht of a friend. And Kate," continued Fenie hurriedly, for Kate had already started, "you needn't be afraid to talk to him, for there are no occupants of those rooms."

Kate tripped out to the piazza and saw Jermyn with a face so sober that it shocked her. She approached him softly and touched his arm; he looked up quickly, but with an entirely different face.

"Am I to go to New York all alone?" Kate asked, with a look which set Jermyn's well-controlled heart dancing, although its owner said,

"What? Your brother, and Mrs. Highwood and Miss Wardlow—aren't they going?"

"You know very well what I mean, you consummate hypocrite."

"And you know very well, or you ought to," said Jermyn, "that I'd gladly follow you all over the earth. Still, I can't force myself upon the remainder of the party."

"Then Trif shall invite you, at once," said Kate.

"Trif," Fenie was saying at almost the same moment, as her sister returned from an unsuccessful search for Trixy, "Kate has gone out to ask Jermyn to accompany us North; wouldn't it be the graceful thing for you, as the head of the party, to add your request to hers?"

"Where is he?" asked Trif. She was on the piazza soon after Fenie told her where the Lieutenant was.

"How kind and thoughtful of you!" said Jermyn. "I suppose," he continued hypocritically, "that I might possibly get permission to be absent a few days longer if——"

"That's all right," intruded the voice of Trixy. "You can go, and that ain't all—you'll get into a lot of trouble if you don't go. I've been to see the head man about it."

"The head man?" echoed Jermyn, while the others looked inquiringly at the child.

"Yes. Don't you know? I mean the man up at the fort, that all you soldiers have to ask when you want to do anything. I told him all about it, although he kept on interruptin', and sayin' 'yes, yes,' as if he wanted me to stop talkin'. I didn't stop, though, so at last he said, 'Little girl, I've already heard something about the matter. Please say to Lieutenant Jermyn, with my compliments, that he is to go to New York at once, and that he isn't to show his face here again for several days, and that if he dares to do so I may have him held to account for getting a leave of absence on false pretenses.' There!—I think I've told it just like he said it, so you see you'll have to go if you don't want to catch it."

"Trixy," exclaimed Jermyn, utterly aghast, "do you mean to say that you have actually called upon the Post Commandant and told him that I was here, and that——"

"Yes, I told him everything I could, so he'd be sure to let you go; told him about your bein' here to lunch with mamma—he looked awful s'prised then, 'cause he thought you'd gone to New York, so I told him what you went for, and how the Admiral brought you back, and then he told me he wished I'd find the Admiral and say he'd be glad to have him come up to the fort to dinner. Then he looked as if he didn't know what to think, and I got afraid that mebbe he'd change his mind and not let you go after all, so I told him that 'twas real important, and about last night up by the lighthouse—don't you remember? Oh, mamma! I promised you real solemn that I wouldn't say a word about that to anybody, didn't I! I wonder how I came to do it?"

Kate looked at Jermyn, and Jermyn blushed; then he looked at Kate, and Kate blushed; as to the others, they looked at both of them and laughed merrily. But Kate wasn't going to let the dear fellow feel uncomfortable, so she said softly—

"You'll go with us?"

"You've heard my orders, my dear, although I must say that they did not come through the customary official channels, but as I got a week's leave last night for this very purpose———"

"You shall have a blissful week," interrupted Trif, "with no one to disturb or make trouble."

"But you forget that the General commanding this department has headquarters at New York, and if Trixy should———"

"Sh—h—" whispered Kate. "That dreadful child might appeal to the President of the United States, in his capacity as commander-in-chief of the army and navy."

"Do be quiet," said Jermyn. "The child is listening with all her might."

# CHAPTER XXI.
## APRIL SHOWERS.

A HAPPIER couple than Fenie and Harry could not be found in all New York. This must be true, for both of them said so one evening while they were the only occupants of Trif's cozy parlor, while Trif and her husband were out, making a short call.

Harry had just told Fenie that while he was very happy about his sister and Jermyn, because he thought them specially suited to each other, he was also very sorry for them, for naturally love could not be so delightful to Jermyn as to him, for was not the officer at least ten years the older. Ten years, to Harry, seemed time enough to transform a young man into a person of middle age.

Fenie said she never would have mentioned such things if Harry had not begun it, but she was dreadfully sorry for Kate, for the dear girl, being much older than she—six or seven years older—could not know the bliss of youth that gives itself entirely to thoughts of love.

Harry did not like to hear any allusions made to the age of his sister, for Kate had always seemed to him, until he met Fenie, the embodiment of everything girlishly delightful. Was she not the merriest romp of the family? Was it not she who always brought him out of his brown studies? Did she not play with the younger children as if she herself was still in short dresses?

By a natural coincidence, Jermyn and Kate, only a few squares away, were congratulating themselves that they were not young things like Harry and Fenie. They had seen much of the world; they knew men and women well; they had gone through many illusions from start to finish, but now they had found each other, the world might move on in its orbit, or out of its orbit, with no end of trouble to all concerned—except them. They were one in soul and purpose for all time, and, they devoutly hoped, for all eternity.

About this time a bell rang somewhere in the house, but neither of them heeded it. Why should they? Were they not sitting and looking as if Jermyn had merely dropped in for an evening call? Kate was pretending to do some alleged "fancy work," and Jermyn was admiring the movements of her pretty hands, and wishing that his pay or his prospects were so good that the aforesaid pretty hands might never have to do anything more exacting or less becoming, and thinking he had been a brute to propose to such a woman when he had only his pay, nearly two thousand a year, and a thousand or two dollars he had saved, when the current of his thoughts was disturbed by the appearance of Trixy, who stood before him in a waterproof cloak and a face covered with tears.

"Trixy!" exclaimed Jermyn. "What has happened to you?"

"They're havin' an awful row," sobbed the child.

"They? Not your father and mother?"

"No, indeed! They never fight—aren't you ashamed of yourself! It's the other two—Aunt Fee and Harry. She says she never loved him much anyhow, and she didn't ask him to go down South and bother her, and he said he didn't believe she knew her own mind, and she said she wished he had any mind worth knowin', and she wished he was half as much of a man as Lieutenant Jermyn, that he'd been abusin'. She said you was a man, and he wasn't nothin' but a boy. And papa and mamma was gone out, and I was awful frightened, and I got the cook to bring me around here, so I could ask Miss Trewman if somethin' couldn't be done for 'em."

"Why should he have abused me?" asked Jermyn of no one in particular.

"Why should she compare him with you?" asked Kate. "Jermyn," she exclaimed, "did you ever make love to Fenie Wardlow?"

"Never! Upon my honor, my dear."

"Then I'm sure I don't know——"

"Neither do I. Suppose I go around with Trixy and find out?"

"I shall go with you," said Kate. There was something in her voice that Jermyn had never heard before, and it distracted his thoughts about Harry and Fenie. Nevertheless the two quickly left the house together, and Jermyn talked to Trixy rather than to Kate, and Kate was made so uncomfortable thereby that she talked incessantly to Trixy, which mystified Jermyn greatly, although Kate's hand grasped his arm tightly all the while.

On their way they chanced to meet Harry, to whom Jermyn said quickly:

"Well met, old chap! Come along with us. We are going to make a call and would like to have you with us; we can promise that you shall have a pleasant time."

"I'd be glad if something pleasant would happen on this particular evening—confound it!" replied Harry in the gruff tone which some very young men, despite good breeding and association, sometimes indulge in. When they reached the Highwoods' house and started up the steps Harry shrank backward and said:

"Not there, thank you. Not this evening."

He started quickly away, but Jermyn, with Kate still clinging to his arm, soon overtook him, grasped his shoulder as a policeman might seize a prisoner, and said, kindly enough:

"My dear fellow, I've seen a score of clever youngsters through lovers' quarrels, and I'm going to see you through one this evening—now, or I'm going to break your neck. Which do you prefer?"

Harry answered nothing, although he acted like a surly criminal led by a jailor. Meanwhile Kate was grasping Jermyn's arm tightly and pressing close to his side. What had become of Trixy no one knew or thought, yet no sooner did they ring the bell than the child stood in the open doorway.

Kate hurried to Fenie's room, where she found the occupant bathed in tears. At any other time such a spectacle would have moved Kate to tenderness, but now she rudely shook the girl and asked:

"Tryphena Wardlow, were you ever in love with Jermyn?"

"No," replied the girl with a wondering blush. "That is———"

"Did he ever make love to you? Tell me—this instant!"

"No. That is———"

"Did he ever kiss you?"

"No, no, no—a thousand times no! Aren't you ashamed of yourself, to have asked such a question?"

"Yes—I am!" said Kate, "and I sincerely beg your pardon, but—here, dear, let me dry your eyes. You poor little darling, has Harry been a brute? Oh, won't I make life miserable for him when I get him alone, at home? There, dear! If your own sister isn't here to comfort you, you shan't lack another. Come down stairs with me; Jermyn is here, and I want you to look your prettiest."

"It isn't necessary," said Fenie, trying to clear her face of the traces of sorrow and anger. "He's no eyes for any one else when you're present."

"You darling girl! Say that again—and again!"

"Old chap," Jermyn was saying to Harry, "I don't know what has been the trouble, but I know the nature of it, for I've seen signs of it in many other men who have been in love. Take all the blame to yourself—do! 'Tis the privilege of men to relieve women of all of that sort of thing they can."

"'Tis very well for you to talk," grumbled Harry. "'They jest at scars that never felt a wound.' But———"

"But, you blessed idiot, do you know what you are in danger of losing? Fenie is one of the sweetest little women on the face of the earth."

"How do you know?" asked Harry defiantly. "Were you ever in love with her? From something she said this evening I am half inclined to——"

"I was in love with her sister, many years ago," said Jermyn softly; "so I know the family quality."

"I beg your pardon," said Harry, humbly, and trying hard to be once more a gentleman. "But she said——"

"'Tis no matter what she said. Be a man; be a lover; be a gentleman. Sh—h—h-!—they're coming."

Kate entered with Fenie, who greeted Jermyn effusively, while Harry chatted with his sister, there being no one else for him to speak to, for Trixy had disappeared. Kate and Jermyn soon succeeded in making the conversation general, and in compelling Harry and Fenie to talk to each other. Then Jermyn and Kate began to admire some of the Highwoods' pictures so intently that Harry and Fenie could talk only to each other; they dropped their voices, but the tones were audible and promised well. Finally, as the others turned they saw something which caused them to say:

"We beg a thousand pardons."

"You needn't," replied Fenie bravely. "We've made up, and I don't care if all the world knows it, for it was all my fault from the first."

"What a fib!" exclaimed Harry.

"It isn't! But how——" here Fenie turned to Kate, "did you chance to come to the rescue? My heart was almost broken."

"And mine," added Harry.

"And mine," said Kate tragically.

"Mine is of no particular consequence," drawled Jermyn, with a reproachful look at Kate, "still, it got a frightful stab."

"You poor fallow!" exclaimed Kate, making amends in the most delightful manner appropriate to the occasion. This demonstration incited Harry and Fenie to be very tender to each other, and there was an instant of delicious silence, too soon broken by a pitiful wail which seemed to come from a portière.

"I s'pose it don't matter about my poor little bit of a heart, but it was broke most to pieces."

"Did that child overhear the quarrel?" whispered Fenie.

"'Twas she who brought us word about it," Kate replied.

Then Harry and Fenie kissed Trixy, and Jermyn took her into his arms, and the child, relieved of her load of responsibility, fell asleep, and Jermyn held her so tenderly and looked at her so fondly and thoughtfully that Kate looked upon him with a new and tender expression in her eyes, although she wouldn't for the world have had him see it. Finally Kate herself took the child, so softly that she did not waken it, and carried it to and fro a moment or two, and finally laid it upon a sofa, and Jermyn looked at Kate every moment, and thought, and thought, and thought. At last he ventured to remark:

"All the artists and poets have been wrong. They should have made Cupid a little girl."

The four sat and talked until Trif and Phil returned, and then they continued to talk, yet the astute heads of the family did not hear or see anything that could make them imagine that there had been any trouble. Indeed, Trif told her husband that it seemed strange that Jermyn and Kate should have spared time for a call on that particular evening, when Jermyn's time was so short, and he must soon be away for no one knew how long.

# CHAPTER XXII.
## "THEY TAKE NO NOTE OF TIME."

KATE and Jermyn were so happy in each other's society, now that they had not to pay attention to a lot of mere acquaintances, that they agreed with the hero of Gilbert and Sullivan's "Mikado" that each second was a minute, each minute an hour, each hour a day, and each day a year. Nevertheless, after the illogical manner of lovers, no sooner was the last half of the week under way than they began to complain that each day seemed only an hour long.

"Must you really go at the end of your week?" asked Kate. "Does a week, in military parlance, mean literally a week—no more, no less?"

"Exactly and mathematically a week," sighed Jermyn. "Tis even worse in our case, for the week includes the time I spent in reaching here, the time I will spend in returning, and the day I started, but was taken back by the Admiral."

"Oh!" exclaimed Kate, after a startled look, "that means that you must start back to-morrow!"

"It does indeed. I've gone over it by every applicable rule of arithmetic, but I can find no other solution."

Kate at once became so dismal that she could not talk much, and Jermyn, remembering the ways of his mother and sisters when they had trouble on their minds, suggested that there could be no better time to make his good-bye call upon the Highwoods; he assured himself that a short chat with sympathetic women would enable Kate to bear her trouble more bravely. He got his reward, for Trif chatted so kindly with him that he himself soon felt much better than he had dared hope, so he felt correspondingly grateful, and wished he might do something in return for the good woman to whose interest he owed so much of his fortune in love. Suddenly there came to him a thought which he voiced at once.

"Mrs. Highwood, I shall go back by way of Washington. I'm greatly your debtor; I needn't go into particulars, but wouldn't you like to spend a few hours in Washington? You couldn't have a better guide than I, and—"

"'Twould be splendid!" Trif exclaimed. "But you wouldn't be so heartless as to leave Kate behind?"

"I'm greatly obliged for the suggestion."

"And," continued Trif, who had been thinking rapidly, "would it be dreadful of me to take Trixy also? She has long been wild to see the 'Baby of the White

House,' and by some lucky accident she might get a peep at that fortunate child."

"It might not be difficult; I've had the honor of meeting the baby's mother, in other years, and am sure she would be delighted to meet a woman like Trixy's mother."

"We will go," said Trif. "I shan't have to wait to consult Phil, for he asked me why I didn't improve my opportunity to see Washington during our return trip from Old Point."

A cheerful party of four started for Washington the next afternoon, and on the morning afterward Jermyn busied himself in showing the ladies the sights of the capital. But Washington is a large city, and time did fly so rapidly—to Kate and Jermyn, for the latter would be obliged to take the night train for Fort Monroe.

Trixy saw the baby of the White House, and devoured it with her eyes, and asked it questions about its dolls, while two fond mothers looked and listened. The call was short, but, as the party made their adieus, Trixy slipped back and said to the lady of the house:

"Your husband can do anything he likes with soldiers, can't he?"

"That depends," was the reply. "Why do you ask?"

"'Cause I wish he would make Lieutenant Jermyn go back to New York with us. I'm sure Miss Trewman wishes so too, 'cause they're only just engaged, and he's only been in New York a week, and———"

"There goes the only man who could manage an affair of that kind," said the lady, pointing to an alert-looking gentleman who was approaching the house.

"Thank you, very much."

"Where is Trixy?" asked Trif, as the party passed through the gateway. "Why, there she is, talking to a stranger! How the child has lost her manners! Mr. Jermyn, won't you kindly bring her back?"

Jermyn hurried to the rescue, and was somewhat astonished to see that the gentleman with whom Trixy was talking was the Secretary of War.

"Mr. Jermyn!" said the Secretary. Jermyn saluted.

"This young lady has been telling me an interesting story. By the way, there are to be some new guns tested at Sandy Hook, New York harbor, in a day or two. It might be of use to some of the classes at the fort if an officer from there were to observe the tests and take back a detailed report. Would your own studies be retarded if you were to remain absent a week or ten days longer?"

"Not in the least," Jermyn replied, with the promptness becoming a soldier.

"Call at the Department some time this afternoon, then, for your detail. I'll send a copy of it to your commanding officer, and you will report by letter to him, so that you may be recalled if necessary. Will you do me the honor to introduce me to this young lady?"

"With pleasure. Miss Highwood, allow me to present the Honorable the Secretary of War."

"What a long name!" exclaimed Trixy, with a curtesy.

"I'm sorry, Miss Highwood, that my time won't allow me to show you special attention while you are here, but I hope we may meet again. Good day. Mr. Jermyn, I wish you a pleasant trip!"


Jermyn hurried the child back to her mother, who said:

"I hope, Mr. Jermyn, that you apologized to the gentleman for Trixy's rudeness?"

"I hadn't the opportunity," Jermyn replied. "Ladies, I've an interesting announcement to make; I am to accompany you back to New York."

"Oh, Jermyn!" exclaimed Kate. "'Tis too good to be true."

"Nevertheless, 'tis as true as it is good. The gentleman with whom Trixy was talking was the Secretary of War, and he has ordered me back, for a few days, on duty that will occupy my time for only a few hours a day."

"You clever fellow! How did you manage it?"

"I didn't. Trixy did it."

"Trixy!" echoed both ladies.

"Why," said the child, "I only told him all about Mr. Jermyn and Miss Trewman. The lady in the White House told me he was the right man to ask if Mr. Jermyn couldn't go back to New York with us, so I asked him." Then Trixy looked up with the inquiring air she always had when she suspected she had done something wrong, but didn't know what it was.

"Bless me!" exclaimed Kate. "I wonder only that she didn't ask the President himself."

"That's what I was goin' to do," explained Trixy, "but the lady said the other man was the right one, so I asked him."

All three adults stopped and stared fixedly at Trixy, at which the child began to cry; so Trif picked her up and kissed her and told her to "never mind," and Kate stooped and kissed her, and when she lifted her head there were tears in her eyes; so Trif looked hurriedly toward the War Department and said it was good for the public sense of propriety and dignity that the Secretary was out of sight, otherwise it would be just like Kate to kiss him also, as she had kissed the Admiral on a certain occasion.

Kate hurried the party away; she explained later that while looking toward the White House she was sure that she saw the hostess looking through the window at her and smiling at her.

"I declare!" she said, with downcast eyes and cheeks a-flame, "there's no living with Trixy, nor——"

"Nor any living without her—eh?" added Jermyn.

The remainder of the day was the very merriest, so four people said, that any party had ever spent in Washington. Jermyn took his guests to the old chamber of the House of Representatives, and mystified them a few moments with the "whispering gallery" over the Speaker's desk, making Kate his latest victim, despite her appeals to him to be quiet, and his assurances that no one else could hear a word he was saying, although he was forty feet away. Kate became so embarrassed that she suddenly withdrew and Trixy took her place—a change which Jermyn did not notice until he heard a peal of childish laughter, and, stepping forward, saw Kate and Trif standing some steps from the arch and Trixy joining them, and saying:

"That's the funniest thing I ever heard of!"

"What is the funniest thing, dear?" asked Trif.

"Trixy," exclaimed Jermyn, "don't tell, please."

"But I must mind mamma," pleaded the child. "Besides——"

"Trixy," exclaimed Jermyn, "if you repeat what I said I'll never speak to you again."

"Trixy," said Kate, "if you don't tell I'll never speak to you again—I mean," for Kate had caught an appealing look from Jermyn—"I won't speak to you if you do tell."

The child was so confused that she did not know what to do, so she turned to her mother for advice, and Trif hurried her a few steps in advance.

"Remember, Trixy!" cried Kate after them.

"Don't forget, Trixy!" shouted Jermyn, in his sternest tone of command.

Two more uncomfortable lovers than Kate and Jermyn were in the next five minutes could not have been found anywhere, for Kate wondered what it was all about and insisted upon knowing, and Jermyn replied that he would tell her at some future time, and Kate wanted to know why he couldn't tell her at once, and Jermyn replied, somewhat sheepishly, that some things might be said in the privacy of a whispering gallery that could not easily be said face to face in a crowded street, upon which Kate wailed:

"But that child heard it!"

"Never mind, my dear; she'll forget it."

"Not she! I'm beginning to believe that the smaller the child the less chance there is of her forgetting what shouldn't be remembered. And, oh, Jermyn! Of all men in the world, here comes Admiral Allison! What if she should tell him?"

"If she does," said Jermyn desperately, "I'll never again dare look him in the face; I shall always believe he is laughing at me. 'Tis all your fault, my dear. If you hadn't made me love you so dearly, I wouldn't have said——"

"Let us overtake them—quick!" said Kate.

"We've been up to the whisp'rin' gall'ry," Trixy was already saying to the Admiral, "and——"

"Trixy!" sternly spoke three voices as one.

"What rare fortunes Providence has in store for old men!" exclaimed the Admiral. "I greatly wanted and needed to see Jermyn, this very day, and I not only find him unexpectedly, but get a couple of glimpses of Paradise beside—yes, three, for here is Trixy also."

"Paradise?" echoed Trixy. "It was somethin' about Paradise that——"

"Trixy!" said Jermyn warningly.

"Allow me," said the Admiral, "to take you all to a hotel, where I may rob you of Jermyn a few moments."

Jermyn took the child's hand, placed himself between her and the Admiral, and thus they walked to the hotel.

---

# CHAPTER XXIII.
## "BEYOND THE DREAM OF AVARICE."

"MY dear boy," said the Admiral, as soon as the party had been comfortably stowed at a hotel, of which officers of the united service are very fond, and after luncheon had been ordered, "don't you want to make your fortune by a few strokes of your pen—or pencil?"

"Admiral," replied Jermyn, "my heart never before warned me so savagely of the condition of my pocket. Fire away."

"Good! Do you remember a conversation we had a few nights ago at the fort with a certain semi-public character about business?"

"A few nights ago?" repeated Jermyn dreamily. "I remember such a talk, but it seems that it was a few months ago."

"Tut, tut! Wake up! This is business—not moonshine."

"I beg your pardon," said Jermyn, quietly rallying himself. "You mean the affair of that gold placer on the Pacific Coast? Do you suppose I ever can forget it, after the misery that came of it, and the trouble you were put to?"

"Never mind me, at present, except to give me your close attention. My dear boy, our suggestions did the business, and Blogsham has more sense of honor than I usually attribute to a business man. Our plans were of so much promise that he has already organized a company to develop the property. The capital is a million dollars, with permission to increase to three millions, and there are at present ten thousand shares of the par value of one hundred dollars each."

"Hem! That sounds business-like, but I don't see how it implies the sense of honor of which you spoke a moment ago."

"What? Oh, to be sure; I've not reached the most important part of the story. Well, the projector writes me that he hasn't forgotten his promise, and that there are five hundred shares of the stock waiting for me, and five hundred for you, which we can have if——"

"No, I've fooled away enough of my hard earnings upon projects of that kind. Excitement of that sort may do for you, on the pay of a rear admiral, retired, but I——"

"Do let me finish, won't you? I wouldn't put a cent into gold-mining, unless I myself were the manager of the concern, if I were a dozen times as well off as I am. But don't you remember Blogsham's promise? We're to have this stock for nothing but the services we have already rendered. Blogsham asks only that the transactions and his assertions to the company may be entirely business-like, that we shall send him for the company's archives, the sketches which gave him his new ideas as to how to make the placer a working success."

"Whew-w-w-w-!" whistled Jermyn. "Will you kindly remember where those sketches are —or where there is every reason to believe they are?"

"Perfectly; nevertheless they must be obtained. Fifty thousand dollars is too much money for either of us to throw away—Blogsham says the stock can already be sold at par. I'm sure that Mrs. Highwood is too much interested in your future welfare to make any objection to giving up the original document."

"You forget that she sent it to her husband."

"Well, he and she are one, aren't they? I should imagine so, from Madam Trif's manner of talking about her lord and master."

"But there was a private letter on the same sheet of paper, which———"

"Which can easily be erased."

"I can't ask it—really I can't," said Jermyn. "I'd rather lose fifty thousand dollars than remind Mrs. Highwood of something that would be embarrassing to think of, in my presence."

"Then ask her by letter, from as far away as you like. It ought to be done at once though, for offers like Blogsham's are too much in air when made only verbally. We must have the sketches. If you won't ask for them I must. My conscience won't let me see a woman like Miss Trewman marry a subaltern with less than two thousand a year. The income of fifty thousand dollars, added to your own salary, will enable you to marry, and support your wife in a manner that she is accustomed to."

Jermyn was in an unpleasant quandary, but he soon got out of it by saying that to ask for the letter would be ungentlemanly of him, so he couldn't do it.


"Then, you stupid fellow," said the Admiral, "I myself shall ask for them— for my own sketch, at least. She already knows that I know the contents of the letter."

"You won't dare remind her of it," exclaimed Jermyn.

"Won't I, though! Indeed I will. I have sufficient excuse. I shall tell her frankly why I want it—that an estimable though obstinate friend of mine is about to marry on an insufficient income, and that I'm so sorry for his wife that I'm going to settle fifty thousand dollars upon her, and that I can't do it unless I regain the sketch which was on the blank half of that letter sheet; your sketch, you'll remember, was on the back of the written portion. Then, if she gives me the entire letter———"

"Which you know she wouldn't do."

"I don't see why not, if I first ask her to erase the writing. Now, my dear boy, I have you at my mercy. You're on your way back to the fort; I will accompany the ladies back to New York, and———"

"Aha! You will, will you?" exclaimed the younger man, with a soldier's instinctive delight at getting an enemy at a disadvantage. "I'm going back to New York with them myself. I've been ordered back, on duty."

"Hem! For how long, may I ask?"

"Well, as you can learn by inquiry at the Department, I may as well tell you that it will be for a week, at the least."

"Suppose, then," said the Admiral, after a moment of thought, "that we agree upon an armistice. You go to New York; so shall I. I shan't annoy you in your special business—never fear—and I'll give you a full week in which to make up your mind, but if by that time you haven't procured those sketches I shall charge myself with the getting of them, no matter how much begging and arguing may be required. Is it agreed?"

"I suppose it must be," said Jermyn. "You well know that I couldn't willingly deprive you of the chance to make fifty thousand dollars, after all you have done for me, you great-hearted old rascal!"

"Not even if I were to give the money to your wife?" said the Admiral, with a world of shrewdness in the sidelong look with which he regarded his companion.

"You know very well that I wouldn't allow you to do such a thing!" replied Jermyn angrily.

"Hurrah!" shouted the Admiral.

By that time the luncheon was ready, and the Admiral made himself delightfully companionable to the ladies, but Jermyn was so silent and abstracted that even Kate rallied him, asking him if the New York duties which the War Department had imposed, compelled such hard thinking? Jermyn replied that they weren't, but that the Admiral had just given him the most provoking lot of orders that one man ever received from another, so both ladies insisted at once upon knowing what the orders were, and both men maintained silence to a degree that was simply maddening, so Kate quizzed Jermyn privately, and he told her, privately, that she mustn't say another word about it. Kate afterward told Trif, in confidence, that she must have been right in supposing that the business upon which the two men had gone North, a few days before, must have been of great importance to the Government, as well as of an extremely secret nature; but that, nevertheless, it was a burning shame that older officers had such despotic control of their juniors, and that if women had charge of government affairs, there would not be any of such manifest injustice.

They all went to New York that night. While Jermyn visited the Department for his order, the Admiral scoured Washington for the projector of the gold mine, who had been in the city the day before, but as the man had already returned to the metropolis, the Admiral intended to be at his elbow, to keep the promise of stock alive until the sketches could be obtained. Should there seem to be any danger, he would promptly break the armistice and ask Trif for the fateful letter.

Suddenly, however, while the two officers were smoking together on the train, Jermyn struck terror to the Admiral's heart by saying:

"Your plan for reclaiming those pictures may be of no good. 'Tis more than likely that Highwood has destroyed that letter."

"My dear boy!" exclaimed the old man. "Please don't imagine anything so dreadful! Destroyed one hundred thousand dollars? Horrors!"

"I think it likely," continued Jermyn, "for at Old Point I chanced to hear Mrs. Highwood say that after carefully reading her husband's letters she always destroyed them, so that no one else by any chance could see them. Like husband, like wife—you know the old saying."

"But you saw the letter in Highwood's own hands," said the Admiral.

"True; but at that time his wife was away, and I suppose he kept all of her letters to look at again and again—I am sure I should do so, if I were married and my wife was away from me."

"Good boy! I'm glad to see that you already know the feeling. Still—if he should have destroyed them!"

It was the Admiral's turn to be strangely silent during the evening, and the ladies marvelled greatly at the change in a man who had seemed to them the life of whatever company he chanced to be in, and Kate found opportunity to whisper to Trif that Jermyn did not seem to be entirely under the Admiral's thumb after all, for he seemed to be in remarkably good spirits—commanding spirits, indeed, she could say.

At a part of the road over which the train passed early in the night, Jermyn begged the ladies to go with him to the rear platform to observe a beautiful moonlight landscape which he knew of old. The Admiral, who remained behind with Trixy, soon began to sketch on the back of a letter. The shrewd old chap had argued to himself that if the letter had really been destroyed there could be nothing dishonorable in duplicating his own sketch on the back of another letter, and offering it in evidence. It would be virtually the same picture, for he would draw it from memory, as before.

He worked so long that Trixy, wishing to do something new, began to look over his shoulder, and soon she exclaimed:

"Why-y-y! I've got a picture just like that."

"You have?" replied the Admiral, carelessly. "That's strange; where did you get it?"

"I tore it off a letter—the back of that letter that came from the fort one day, for you, don't you know, and I opened it by mistake while I was——"

The Admiral dropped pencil and paper, placed his hands upon Trixy's shoulders, and exclaimed:

"You have that picture? Where?"

"Why, in my scrap-book, at home."

"Fifty thousand dollars saved!" shouted the Admiral. He was anything but silent when the ladies returned; indeed, he talked so incessantly that Trif had to break in upon one of his best stories by pleading that she must remove some of the dust of travel before leaving the train at New York.

# CHAPTER XXIV.
## TRICKS UPON TRIXY.

AFTER reaching New York the Admiral lost no time in calling at the Highwoods, and although he tried to appear at his best, Fenie said to her sister in strict confidence that there must be something about sea air which specially suited veteran sailors, for the Admiral did not seem the same man he had been at Old Point. He was genial, courteous, conversational, witty, but there was a certain indefinable something lacking; after much study, the girl concluded that the difference came of a strange absent-minded manner which appeared to possess him once in a while, for no apparent reason.

As the old gentleman had spent but a single hour at the Highwoods when this sage conclusion was announced, Trif called her sister a goose, and said she had been carrying Harry in her mind so long that she was incapable of judging other men with any degree of fairness. Nevertheless, Trif told her husband that the Admiral did not seem entirely himself.

The truth was that the old gentleman chanced to call at an hour when Trixy was calling upon a juvenile acquaintance a few squares away, and as she was at the age when children never know when to go home unless they are sent away or sent for, the Admiral was unable to accomplish the real purpose of his visit, which was to see Trixy's scrap-book. He went away with about as uncomfortable a mind as you or I might have, dear reader, were fifty thousand dollars almost within our grasp, yet with a child's caprice and carelessness somewhere between it and full possession.

The Admiral rested badly that night, but he awoke in the morning with a capital plan of operations. He went to a bookstore and purchased a large assortment of illustrated papers, American and foreign, and sent them to his hotel. Then he made a morning call at the Highwoods, just for a moment, to ask if he might not take Trixy to walk with him. The child was delighted, especially when the old gentleman took her to his hotel and showed her all his picture papers, and asked her whether she would not like to spend the following morning with him, and bring her scrap-book, so that he and she might paste into it all the pictures she might select from his papers.

Success being thus assured, his spirits returned in full force, so that after he called on Kate Trewman in the afternoon Kate herself hurried around to the Highwoods to tell them that she had never before found the Admiral such delightful company, and that evidently there was nothing like a trip to New York to brighten any one's wits. Trif and Fenie were mystified, and after Kate's departure they agreed that there must be something in advancing years that made men variable in spite of themselves.

The Admiral lay in wait for Jermyn, who was to dine with him that evening after returning from the gun-proving grounds, and he tormented the young man so unmercifully about the letter that Jermyn wished he had dined alone. The Admiral could afford to be playful, for was he not sure of getting at least one of the pictures?

The next morning bright and early he called for Trixy and her scrap-book, and gallantly insisted upon relieving her of the weight of the book itself; with the precious volume in his hand he felt as if the stock certificates were already in his possession. He hurried the child to his hotel, heartlessly passing several candy shops and two soda-water places, until some pointed remarks brought him to a proper sense of the courtesies due to very young ladies who walk with gentlemen of mature years.

Trixy's tongue, never inactive for many moments at a time, was entirely loosened by the gratifying flavors imparted to it by the Admiral's kindness, so its owner soon began to talk of the two subjects which were uppermost in home conversation.

"Say," she asked, "Mr. Jermyn don't have to be killed until there is a war, does he?"

"No indeed, my dear, nor even if there should be a war. What put so dreadful an idea into your head?"

"Oh, only that mamma says it would be so dreadful when Miss Trewman loves him so much. Besides, mamma says it would be dreadful hard in another way, 'cause the Trewmans ain't rich. They used to be, but their father lost a lot of money in business a few years ago, and papa says he hasn't got it back yet."

The Admiral quickly lost his compunctions of conscience about the trick he intended to play, which was to abstract the original sketch from Trixy's scrap-book during the clipping and pasting operations at the hotel, and substitute the imitation which he had made on the train. It had seemed an ungentlemanly and under-handed thing to do, much though he informed himself that the result would not injure the child in any way. Now, after what Trixy had told him about the condition of the Trewman finances, it would be a matter of absolute duty. Still more, he would fulfil the threat he had made to Jermyn, in case Jermyn's own sketch could not be recovered. He could not do it all at once, of course; Jermyn's pride would never allow it, but he would make the bride a handsome present in government bonds on her wedding day, and he would bequeath the remainder of the fifty thousand to her in his will, and should the fortunes of war or peace take Jermyn from earth before him, he would see that the remainder of the money should reach the widow at once. With such virtuous and unselfish resolves, what harm could there be in plundering a small girl's scrap-book?

"Papa says," continued Trixy, "that there is no sense in worryin' about it, 'cause both of 'em are so fond of each other that they'd marry for love even if they had to starve afterward."

"Hem! Quite likely. I suspect I would, if I were either of them."

"Is that so? I must tell mamma that, 'cause p'raps it will keep her from worryin'. Papa says she worries too much about her friends' affairs."

"Er—my dear, I wouldn't say anything about it, if I were you; for maybe your parents might not like to think that you had been repeating any of their conversation."

It took considerable effort on the part of the Admiral to prevent any farther disclosures, and the old gentleman was very glad when he reached the hotel, and an examination of the pictorial papers gave the child something new to talk about. The Admiral had scissors and paste ready, and allowed Trixy to clip at will while he endeavored to rob the scrap-book. He lost no time in turning the pages, but a hasty examination failed to disclose the sketch which represented fifty thousand dollars, so he looked again, with extreme care. Toward the end his heart sank, and at the last page he uttered a low groan.

"What's the matter?" asked Trixy, looking up from her work.

"I beg a thousand pardons, my dear. I merely gave way, for an instant, to a bad habit into which old gentlemen sometimes fall. How are you getting along? Oh, you're finding a capital lot, aren't you? Don't you want to stop a moment or two, and show me your book?"

Trixy began at once to turn the leaves, and to tell the story of each picture. The Admiral listened patiently as long as he could, but soon he said:

"Won't you show me the one that is like the sketch I made on the train the day we returned from Washington?"

"Certainly." Trixy turned the pages rapidly, but suddenly stopped and looked puzzled; then she exclaimed:

"Somebody's hooked it, I do believe!"

"Oh, don't say that!" said the Admiral, in a shaky voice. "Look again; perhaps you have pasted some other picture over it."

"No I didn't. I know just where I had it in the book; it was right here, by the picture Aunt Fee made of some of the sand hills behind the fort, because they were the only two drawin's I had. And now there ain't nothin there!"

The Admiral looked carefully at the page. Evidently something had been pasted there, and with childish lavishness of mucilage. It could not have dropped out, for bits of paper still adhered to the page. It was plain that some one had carefully removed the sketch.

"Trixy," said the Admiral, as a suspicion came into his mind, "have you ever shown this book to Lieutenant Jermyn?"

"No, never. He ain't ever at our house long enough for me to show him anything."

"Have you loaned the book to any other little girl, or exchanged pictures with any one?"

"No, indeed! Besides, I was keepin' that picture real careful, to remind me of somethin'—mamma told me to. She told me that whenever I looked at that picture I must remember to never again take any writin' from her portfolio and ask other people to finish it for me. I'd just like to know what's happened to that picture; I'm goin' to ask ev'rybody about it as soon as I get back home."

"Oh, don't, please," said the Admiral hastily, "or you'll make me very unhappy."

"What for?"

"Oh, I should dislike to have your father and mother and aunt annoyed about so slight a matter—so far as I am concerned; and you wouldn't have thought of it, you know, if I hadn't spoken of it."

"But they wouldn't be annoyed, and p'raps one of 'em knows where the picture is."

"Eh? Which of them?" The old gentleman looked keenly over the tops of his glasses as a new thought came to him.

"Why, papa, I guess, 'cause he's got a picture a good deal like it on the back of a letter that mamma wrote him, and I saw him lookin' real hard at it the other day, and I asked him what 'twas about, and he said, 'Oh, nothin'.'"

"Aha!"

"What did you say?"

"Did I say something? I must have been merely clearing my throat."

"What a funny lot of noises you do make this mornin'. Well, I guess I'll paste some pictures in the book."

The Admiral lit a cigar, an indulgence of which he never was guilty before dinner, except when laboring under severe mental excitement. One thing at least seemed clear; the letter, with Jermyn's sketch, had not been destroyed; therefore he, the Admiral, could hope to get it, for men knew better than women the value of fifty thousand dollars, and they would forgive other men for asking pointed questions under the circumstances.

But had Phil the Admiral's own sketch? If so, why had he taken it from the book? Merely to tease Trixy? Scarcely.

Suddenly the Admiral smote his forehead and muttered to himself:

"How stupid of me. Mrs. Highwood herself removed that picture. She knew that her daughter had it; she knew the history of it, for I told her all, and she can scarcely have forgotten it. She has a woman's natural delicacy, bless her, about the incident being recalled to my mind, so knowing that Trixy was to bring the book to my room she has abstracted the sketch so that I should not see it and be reminded of a mortifying experience. Oh, woman, woman! How you do keep alive the human tenderness that man does so much to kill!"

Suddenly, however, the Admiral sprang to his feet and exclaimed:

"What if, to make assurance doubly sure, she has destroyed that sketch!"

# CHAPTER XXV.
## THREE BLIND MICE.

FROM that time forward the Admiral was a persistent caller at the Highwoods, for he could not regain his natural composure until he had seen and questioned Phil. The first evening he called Phil had gone out to dinner with some old classmates, and as the Admiral said nothing of the purpose of his visit there was nothing to prevent Phil from remaining late at his office the next night.

All the while, too, Jermyn, whom the Admiral met daily at breakfast, carried himself with an air of bravado which was in the highest degree exasperating. Was it possible that the fellow had himself secured those sketches in some way, and was having a malignantly delightful time in torturing an old man who had been his best friend? It did not seem possible, so one morning the Admiral cautiously remarked:

"By the way, have you done anything about those sketches?"

"Not a thing."

"You don't know anything about them?"

"No more than when we first came North."

"When do you intend to find out?"

"Never, if there's no way but the one you have suggested."

"I don't wonder," said the Admiral icily, "that you're willing to lose your share of the money, for a man in love is generally fool enough to think that he, and particularly his wife, can live on air, but———"

"Admiral!"

"Oh, be angry, if you like, but I mean it. On the other hand, do you think it is conduct becoming an officer and gentleman to deprive me of a lot of money when I've several times put myself to great inconvenience, out of unselfish regard for you?"

"I'd do almost anything in the world to oblige you, Admiral," replied Jermyn, "but after what you've said regarding what you might do with your share of the money, you can't blame me for being reluctant."

"See here, dear boy," pleaded the Admiral, "I'll withdraw that threat if you'll get merely your own sketch. I'll cheerfully lose my own share, if I may feel entirely comfortable about your future."

That shot told. Jermyn could not endure the thought of any man playing martyr for him, so he answered somewhat sulkily:

"I must do it."

"Good! When?"

"Very soon."

"Time is precious, dear boy." Then the Admiral told of his plan regarding Trixy's scrap-book, and his defeat, and finally asked:

"Don't you suppose you could make another sketch of the surroundings of that placer as you did at the fort?"

"Easily."

The Admiral hastily offered the back of a letter and a pencil, and followed with his eyes each mark that Jermyn made. When the sketch was almost complete, Jermyn stopped and asked:

"Why do you want this, Admiral?"

"For use as a voucher, in case your original should be lost."

"Oh, that would be a forgery!"

"Nonsense! Can a man forge his own signature? What would you say in answer to that question, if you were member of a court-martial?"

"I scarcely know," replied Jermyn slowly, "but—" here he paused long enough to tear the paper into strips, and tear the strips crosswise, "I must give my honor the benefit of the doubt."

"Oh, you idiot," exclaimed the old gentleman angrily. "You're worse than an idiot, for you're intimating that I, an officer and gentleman, am counselling a crime."

"Forgive me, Admiral. You know very well that I couldn't, for an instant, think such a thing. Still, any man must be ruled by his own conscience."

Jermyn went down to the Sandy Hook proving-grounds, and the Admiral spent a miserable day, relieved somewhat by a call upon Kate, to whom he determined to tell the whole story, and to appeal to her, first for Jermyn's sake and then for his own, to help him to get those sketches. He knew women, he thought; Kate was a young woman of unusual balance of mind, so she probably had been sensible enough to wonder on what she and Jermyn would live after they married. They would soon marry, the Admiral was sure;

for love, like many other disturbances to which humanity is subject, acts most powerfully where longest delayed or avoided.

But, alas, for human courage! The veteran who had led boarding parties and storming parties, could not muster sufficient courage to tell a woman that another woman had been bent upon making a match for her, and that two men, one of whom was the young woman's own lover, had seen the plan in black and white, while Kate herself had no thought of ever becoming Mrs. Jermyn.

So he called again at the Highwoods, made a full confession to Trif and her husband, and begged for the sketches. Fortunately, the couple were alone, Harry and Fenie having gone to a dinner which the Trewmans were giving to both happy couples. Phil seemed greatly amused by the story, and said:

"So that explains the mystery of those two pictures!" Then, for the first time, he told Trif of meeting Jermyn in Madison Square, and of Jermyn's strange embarrassment on seeing one of the pictures, and how Phil himself had chanced to see the other, only two or three days before the Admiral's call, in Trixy's scrap-book, extracted it, and put the two together to make a pretense of mystery some evening for Trif's bewilderment and his own amusement.

"You dreadful fellow!" exclaimed Trif. "The idea of you keeping a secret from me—and for three whole days!"

"But, pardon me," said the Admiral, "do either of you find it impossible to forgive me?"

"On the contrary," replied Phil, "it is impossible to see where you were to blame. Trixy herself took the letter to you and asked you to finish it, so you couldn't help reading it. Neither could you help supposing it to be what she thought it, her own letter, for it began 'Dear Old Papa.'"

"But," persisted the Admiral, "I was guilty, shamefully so, that in my absent-mindedness I took it from my pocket at the club, to sketch upon."

"Just as I frequently use letters to figure upon," said Phil.

"Thank you—thank you. And poor Jermyn, in making his own sketch, and knowing, of course, the subject of conversation, looked at the written portion, supposing it to be something pertinent to the subject."

"Quite naturally, and each of you afterward had a lot of trouble which he didn't in the least deserve."

"I don't see," said Trif, "that anyone is to blame but I. The experience teaches me never again to leave a letter unfinished."

"Thank you, my dear," said Phil. "You see, Admiral, that your loss is to be my gain. Hereafter I'm not to be disappointed when longing for letters."

"What letters, papa?" asked Trixy from the sitting-room, where she was conducting a spelling lesson for dolls.

"None, dear—tis nothing that you would understand."

"If there is no feeling against me, therefore," said the Admiral, adhering to the purpose of his call, "would you mind, after erasing Mrs. Highwood's lines, giving the sketches to me?"

"It will give me the greatest pleasure to place them in your hands," said Phil, taking some papers from the pocket of his coat. "Why, they're not here! Hem! Ah, I remember; I changed some papers hurriedly this morning to my coat at the office, and apparently those were among them. I'll get them to you tomorrow, and leave them at your hotel as I come up town."

"I shall be there to receive them," said the Admiral, putting on a look of resignation. "Excuse my eagerness and anxiety in the matter, but those sketches have become a veritable nightmare to me."

"I don't wonder," said Phil, "considering what they represent. Trixy, dear, don't laugh so loud. What is the matter?"

"Oh, I'm tellin' the dolls somethin' funny, and I have to do the laughin' for the whole lot of them, don't you see?"

"Bless the child!" exclaimed the Admiral. "Don't check her, please. I wonder if the dolls would think it an intrusion if I were to look on?"

"Phil!" said Trif, suddenly.

"Yes, my dear."

"Do you want to please me very much?"

"You know I do."

"Then go down to your office to-night for those sketches—it isn't yet late enough for the janitor to be asleep. I'm sure that our friend the Admiral, will sleep much easier when he has those pictures securely in his possession."

"Oh, I couldn't think of putting you to such trouble," said the Admiral quickly, although he told himself that Trif was a woman of a million. Trif insisted, and begged the Admiral to wait until Phil's return. It seemed to the old gentleman that every minute of Phil's absence would be an hour long, yet under Trif's influence the minutes passed almost as quickly as seconds, so before long Phil's step was heard in the hall. Trif and the Admiral instinctively arose, but to their surprise they saw a very blank face as Phil exclaimed:

"'Tis the most provoking thing that ever happened. Those sketches are nowhere in the office."

"What can have become of them?" murmured Trif.

"I've not the faintest idea. Here are some more papers that were in the same pocket."

"'Foiled again,' as the villain always says in a melodrama," remarked the Admiral; "kindly consider me the villain." The old gentleman was trying to make light of his disappointment, but he looked so grave that Phil hastened to say:

"I assure you, Admiral, that the sketches can not possibly have been lost, nor can any one have stolen them. I shall make thorough search for them at once, and give myself no peace until I have found them."

"I beg that you won't put yourself to any inconvenience," said the Admiral. Nevertheless, he made haste to take his departure, hoping that the search would begin at once and continue through the night, unless the missing papers were sooner found.

"I shall carry them to you, in person, as soon as I get them," were Phil's parting words.

"Come at any hour," replied the Admiral. "Don't fear that you may disturb me."

Then he went to his hotel, and hopefully, fearfully, remained awake until and through the "dog watch" hours, but in vain.

# CHAPTER XXVI.
## THE OTHER COUPLE.

AS Harry and Fenie had no prospective fortunes complicated by scraps of paper in another man's pocket, they had every reason to be entirely happy, yet soon they found themselves very much to the contrary. Fenie had begun early, like a loyal wife that was to be, to tell Harry of everything that was on her mind, and Harry, like a good brother, began to be concerned about his sister's prospects. The family fortunes were not in as bad condition as Trixy had led the Admiral to fear, but what loving brother could be entirely cheerful while his sister was in danger of losing fifty thousand dollars?

He began to be absent-minded at home, and Kate quickly noticed it, and asked him what was the matter, and when he replied, "Nothing," he did it in a tone that whatever was the matter was the reverse of nothing, so she set herself to discovering what it could be. She at once assumed that it was trouble of some sort between him and Fenie, and she determined to rectify it, no matter what it might be. They were mere children, Harry and Fenie, in Kate's estimation, and would need her sisterly care and supervision until they were safely married.

With the best of intentions she called upon Fenie to find out all about it, and she found the girl in a state of high excitement, for she had been helping Trif to search every place in the house where those awful sketches could possibly have been put, for Phil, like many another man, was an adept at dropping the contents of his pockets in unexpected places. Kate was thinking of nothing but the business on which she had come, so she proceeded promptly to business.

"Harry seems quite unhappy," she began bluntly. "He is entirely unlike his usual merry self."

"Indeed?" replied Fenie vacantly.

"Yes; he looks as if he had slept scarcely a wink last night."

"Pshaw!" exclaimed Fenie with a slight frown.

Kate was somewhat provoked at this, but she controlled herself and continued:

"I asked him what was troubling him, but he wouldn't tell me, although he has always made me his confidant."

Fenie looked uncomfortable, but she showed no sign of becoming communicative, so Kate went on:

"Don't you suppose I would be of any service to you or him in the matter?"

"Not in the slightest degree," said Fenie, with a start. She was thinking only of the ridiculousness of Kate assisting at the work of rummaging the pockets of the various garments which Phil had worn since he missed the sketches, but Kate naturally failed to imagine that, so she misconstrued the gesture.

"I do hope, dear," she said, as sympathetically as she could, "that it isn't anything serious!"

"But it is," said Fenie, looking as if she would like the subject dropped. For that very reason Kate clung to it determinedly.

"Serious?—for two people who ought to love each other very dearly?"

"Yes," replied Fenie bluntly. She was afraid to say much, for, if she gave Kate any clue to the matter, she did not know how much further she might be persuaded to go. She knew that her tongue sometimes ran away with her, and she was not going to let Kate know anything about the missing letter and its double contents.

Suddenly Trif, who did not know that there was a visitor in the parlor, called Fenie, and the girl, glad of an excuse, hurried away with the promise that she would return in a moment. When, however, she explained to her sister, Trif told her she was very silly not to see that Kate was misunderstanding matters, and supposing there was trouble between Fenie and Harry.

"But," said Fenie, "as she already knows that it concerns a couple who ought to love each other very dearly—those were her own words—she will think there is something wrong between her and Jermyn, or between you and Phil." Trif was perplexed by this view of the matter, so she and her sister set themselves to devise some way of throwing Kate off the scent, and, as neither of them had any experience in deceit, they evolved and discarded several plans in rapid succession.

Kate was becoming restive. She had a woman's sense of the courtesy that was due her, and she began to feel hurt by what seemed to be neglect. Just then Trixy meandered into the parlor, from nowhere in particular, and Kate had no scruples about questioning her.

"Trixy, dear," she said, "I'm very glad to see you."

Trixy indulged in a long stare before she replied:

"That's funny! You don't look as if you was."

"Don't I? I'm very sorry for it. The truth is, I'm greatly troubled about several things. I'm afraid, for one thing, that Harry and Fenie aren't as happy as they have been."

"I guess you're right," was the reply, "though I wouldn't have thought of it if you hadn't said so. They talked awful solemn to each other last night. I don't know what they was talkin' about, but once Harry put his hands all over his face and said: 'Oh, 'twill be awful—awful!'"

"Dear me! And what did your Aunt Fee say?"

"She didn't say nothin' for a long time, and then she said she thought he was makin' altogether too much fuss about it."

"About what?"

"I don't know, except she said somethin' about Mr. Jermyn bein' a real fine fellow anyway, so she thought Harry ought to be quiet, and make the best of it."

Jermyn! Aha! Harry was jealous! How much cause had he? If any, then she, Kate, had quite as much. Oh, the ways of very young women! Was Fenie's head still turned by the attention which Jermyn had paid her at Old Point? Had she really lost her heart to him? Was she tiring of Harry, and wishing she might yet capture the officer? Jermyn had admitted to Kate that he had been greatly impressed by Fenie until she, Kate, herself appeared on the scene, but it couldn't be possible that he——

"Trixy?" said Kate suddenly, "does Lieutenant Jermyn come here often?" She was ashamed of herself as soon as she had spoken, for when could he call? Was he not at the proving-grounds all day, and at Kate's own home every evening until late? Still, the question had been asked, so she awaited the answer.

"Why, no. He came here this mornin', very early, and——"

"And your mamma saw him?"

"No, mamma was out."

"So you entertained him?"

"No, I didn't either. I wanted to, 'cause I like him lots, but he and Aunt Fee began talkin' about a letter, and then Aunt Fee told me to get all my new dolls to show him, now that they've all got new dresses, and it took me a lot of time to get them all together, and when I came back with 'em he was gone."

Kate was angry, but of one thing she informed herself at once—it was that she was not going to lose Bruce Jermyn because of any flirtation he might have had with that flighty girl, or of any letters that might have passed between them. Men would be flirts, she supposed—that is, bachelors would—but she would marry Bruce Jermyn, even if he had flirted with half the women in creation. She had long cherished the fine belief that no man ever strays from a woman who appreciates him; when she became Mrs. Jermyn she would be everything to him that wife could be to husband, and then she would defy anyone, even a girl as pretty as Fenie, to get and keep a bit of his heart.

As to Fenie, it would break Harry's heart to lose her, and if temptation were out of her way she probably would love Harry sincerely after they were married. Jermyn would be out of the way in a day or two,—but, oh, how she did wish she knew what was in the letter which the two had talked about?

Fenie finally returned and Kate said to her:

"You expect Harry this evening, I suppose?"

"Oh, yes, I suppose so."

"I hope you will have a very pleasant evening with each other."

"Oh, so do I. I hope it will be pleasanter than last evening. If that dreadful let——"

Fenie stopped abruptly, but it was too late. Kate was regarding her searchingly, and Fenie's face became scarlet.

"What letter do you refer to?"

"Oh, don't ask, please." Fenie felt that she should scream.

"A letter which has made much unhappiness for you and Harry?"

"Yes; yes; oh, yes!" Fenie looked so miserable that Kate almost forgave her. After all, was she not a mere girl? Perhaps a womanly word, spoken in season, might do her good, beside providing peace for Kate's own mind in the future. So she began:

"I believe you're real sorry about it."

"Oh, indeed I am; sorrier than I can begin to tell you."

"Then, dear," said Kate, compelling a genuine pardoning spirit to take possession of herself, "try to think no more about it, no matter what the contents of the letter may be. Let bygones be bygones. Some things must be lived down, if we are to be all we should. Do your share toward it, and all may yet be well."

"But you—and Jermyn—"

So Jermyn really was implicated! Nevertheless, Kate set her lips firmly and replied:

"Jermyn shall live it down; I shall never recall the matter to his attention, but shall do all in my power to make him forget the letter."

"But," said Fenie, with a wondering look, "how did you chance to know anything about it?"

"Never mind about that. You still love Harry, don't you?"

"Indeed, yes!"

"And you will show him that letter—after you are married?"

"Why, yes—if it is ever found."

Kate wanted one more proof of Fenie's repentance; it was a hard one to exact, but she was determined to have it.

"You will show the letter to me too?"

"Yes—after you are married, and if you'll promise to forgive us."

"I do promise—now!" said Kate, and departed with the air of one who had done a noble deed, while Fenie hurried to Trif and told her that Kate already knew about that letter, despite all that had been done to keep any knowledge of it from her, and Trif wondered how she could have learned, and said that Harry must have told her, and Fenie retorted that Harry was no tell-tale child, and that it must have been Jermyn or the Admiral, and that whichever it was he was real mean, for hadn't Trif, while writing the letter, planned merely what had come to pass, to the manifest delight of the parties most nearly interested?

Kate improved her first opportunity to warn her brother against long engagements, and Harry asked whether she herself was willing to practice what she preached, and Kate bravely answered that she was.

"But let that subject rest, for the present," she said. "I've learned some things accidentally to-day, and I don't wonder that you have been so unhappy for a day or two. You needn't be afraid to call on Fenie this evening. There will be nothing unpleasant."

"My dear sister!" exclaimed Harry, "what are you talking about? What have you learned, and where, and how?"

"Entirely by accident. Trixy——"

"Trixy? Goodness! Will that child never cease to make trouble?"

Then Harry dashed out of the room.

# CHAPTER XXVII.
## THREE DAYS GRACE.

THE Admiral worried himself almost sick over Phil Highwood's inability to find the missing sketches, and his condition of mind and body was not improved by a meeting which he had with the projector of the new mining company. That gentleman insisted that the sketches should be filed at once, for his promise from his fellow-incorporators had been merely verbal, and he warned the Admiral that such promises were frequently ignored in business, and that he, the projector, would be powerless to force the matter should his associates vote against him.

The Admiral explained the cause of the delay and the importance of the matter to Jermyn in particular, and this affected the projector so strongly, he once having been a poor young man engaged to be married, that he succeeded in exacting from the directors a written promise that if the sketches were deposited with the company within three days from date the stock should be delivered; otherwise it would be disposed of elsewhere.

All this caused the old gentleman to once more speak to Jermyn about the matter, and Jermyn, noting the condition to which excitement had brought his friend, and not knowing that the Admiral had already made a clean breast of the matter to the Highwoods, one morning went to throw himself upon Trif's mercy, but, as already intimated, he saw only Fenie. He succeeded in telling her the story, but when he learned that the sketches had disappeared he became about as miserable as the Admiral.

Had he spoken when first the sketches were asked for, there would have been no trouble, he learned; he therefore reproached himself severely for his friend's sake and for Kate's, and began wondering how he could ever make amends to the man who had done so much for him. As an army officer's opportunities for making fifty thousand dollars are practically non-existent, he became so moody that Kate thought her suspicions about him and Fenie were verified.

But Kate was not going to lose a happy evening from the short remainder of Jermyn's leave of absence, as she persisted in calling his assignment to duty at Sandy Hook. As she was going to be magnanimous, and had begun finely, she resolved to complete the task, so she exclaimed to Jermyn suddenly one evening:

"My dear boy, I want you to stop thinking about that letter. Don't start—nor ask me any questions. I'll promise to overlook it, and forget all about it, in the course of time, if you will be your old self once more."

"But I never can forget it," replied Jermyn, "never! Think of the cruelty of it, to you?"

"But if I ignore it, and cast it from my mind forever, why should you persist in cherishing it and being miserable about it?"

"Why? Because I am a man and love you."

"I shall love you the more, because you have been so miserable about the matter. Won't that satisfy you?"

How grand a woman she was, Jermyn thought! Still, how could she have learned about that letter, and the drawings that made it so valuable? Had the Admiral told her, and asked her to add her entreaties to his own? Trif could not have been the informer; she had every reason for avoiding the subject, in conversation with Kate. Kate had said he must not ask her how she learned about the tormenting paper; but suddenly he found out, or thought he did, for Kate said:

"Will it make your mind any easier to know that I have fully forgiven her?"

"Then you really know all?" said he, looking into her eyes. He did it very coolly, in the circumstances, Kate thought, but she was not going to recede a bit from the greatness of magnanimity upon which she had resolved, so she said:

"Yes, all; but why should I harbor any ill feeling? Besides, she is quite weak and silly. She will know more when she grows older."

"I am sorry to hear you speak of her in that way," said Jermyn, gravely. "I had hoped that you and she would become very warm friends; indeed, I supposed you were so already."

Kate darted a suspicious look at Jermyn. Was there duplicity in a man apparently so honest? If so, her faith in human nature would be forever lost.

"Why do you wish us to be warm friends?" she asked, coldly. "So that you may frequently have her near you?"

Jermyn looked amazed and indignant as he exclaimed:

"Kate, I swear to you that the tender regard I once had for her is gone forever. Do believe me."

"Then it was not you who wrote the letter about which you and she have been so troubled about in the last few days?"

"I? Why, you said you knew all about it! Don't you know that she wrote it?"

"The forward minx!"

"I thought you said you had forgiven her?"

"I wish I hadn't! The idea of a girl as careful as Fenie Wardlow professes to be——"

"My dear girl, you've been dreadfully misinformed in some way. Fenie didn't write the letter; 'twas her sister."

"Jermyn!" exclaimed Kate, utterly aghast. What was the world coming to? She had heard of married women who pretended to adore their husbands, and who intrigued with other men, but she supposed they were far from the society in which she moved. So it was Trif and her—carelessness, call it, over which Fenie had been so uncomfortable when Kate called, a few hours back! Oh, the wickedness of the world! Whom now was there to trust?

"So," said Kate, slowly and coldly, "it was a married woman, one whom I have respected and loved, who wrote you the letter which——"

"Stop, Kate—at once. There is a dreadful mistake somewhere. Let us be entirely frank with each other, for the good of all concerned. The only letter about which I have had any discomfort is one which Mrs. Highwood wrote to her own husband."

"Her own husband!" echoed Kate, with a blank stare.

"Yes. Let us begin at the beginning, and get your mind out of this dreadful tangle. Do tell me from whom, and how, you got your information about that unspeakably troublesome letter?"

"From Trixy," answered Kate, feebly; at which Jermyn laughed heartily before he replied:

"I might have imagined it. The little marplot! Now listen: the letter is one which Mrs. Highwood wrote her husband, from Old Point, on two subjects, one of which was very delightful, for it was you; I was the other. By an accident, which I will explain later, the letter fell into the Admiral's hands, and he, not distinguishing it from several others which he took from his pocket an hour or two afterward, made a sketch upon the back of it; I, who chanced to be with him, made another. Both sketches are now needed, at once, to perfect some business arrangements in which the Admiral and I are greatly interested and by which we might profit greatly, but Highwood, to whom his wife sent the letter when she regained it, has mislaid the sheet, or the two parts of it, and the Admiral and I, as well as the entire Highwood family, are greatly troubled about it."

"So is Harry and Fenie," said Kate, as if talking to herself. "What an idiot I have been! How they will laugh at my expense! But oh, I am so happy, although I don't deserve to be, for I have been jealous, suspicious, hateful——"

"Do restrain yourself, my dear girl."

"I've also been meddlesome," Kate continued, "and impertinent, and, worse than all, inexpressibly stupid, on account of that dreadful letter. Meanwhile, I am being heartless, for you said the loss of the letter was making trouble for you and the Admiral. How much is the trouble—to you?"

"Oh, merely fifty thousand dollars worth."

"Jermyn! I supposed that I had promised to marry an army officer with nothing but his salary, and I was priding myself on marrying for love alone, without any of the sordid ideas which fill women's heads, as well as men's, in these selfish days, but you seem——"

"Don't change your mind, I beg, for I am fully as poor as you thought me. I expect to be fifty thousand dollars better off if that letter with my sketch comes to light within a few hours; otherwise my entire fortune is the couple of thousand dollars I have saved."

Kate smiled bravely and sweetly as she replied:

"Please don't omit me, while you're giving an account of your possessions. Not that I have any money, but——"

"Bless you!" exclaimed Jermyn, with the demonstration appropriate to the circumstances. There was a short silence, which Kate broke by saying:

"I wonder what was in that letter about you and me."

Jermyn did not answer.

"Do you know?" Kate asked.

"Yes."

"Then tell me."

"I can't, my dear—really I can't."

"Do you think it right that either of us should keep anything from the other?"

"No; but a communication from a husband to his wife belongs only to the two—Mr. and Mrs. Highwood."

"Never mind. I shall know it all some day. Fenie promised that I should."

"Indeed? When is she to tell you?"

"After I am married."

"And you are very, very curious to know?"

"Wildly so!"

"I can see but one way to assist you."

"What is it?"

"Can't you imagine?"

"No. Do tell me—at once."

Jermyn took her hands in his and replied:

"'Tis only this; get married as soon as possible. I shall soon be entitled to ask for two more weeks of absence, and then——"

"I shall be ready," said Kate softly, yet with a look which made Jermyn wonder how much happier a man could be without losing his senses.

"One thing I must do at once, though," said Kate, suddenly regaining her alertness and self-control. "I must apologize abjectly to Fenie for my shameful suspicion that she had been engaged in a flirtation with you. I must do it this very evening. Please take me around there at once."

"And rob myself of one of my few remaining hours of bliss?"

"You must learn to be blissful while doing whatever I wish you to do."

Fenie was so surprised by the communication which Kate made that she did not think to be indignant; on the contrary, she laughed, which was the worst punishment she could have inflicted. Meanwhile, Trif was telling Jermyn that he and Kate must take dinner with her and Phil the next night. The other happy couple would be present, so would the Admiral, and the dinner would be the finest she had ever arranged.

"Yes," said Trixy, "there's to be ice-cream, and the other kind of ice, and mamma says I can eat a lot of both; and there's to be a s'prise, too."

Trif nodded warningly at Trixy. She could not remember which of her prospective dishes had been alluded to in family conversation as a surprise, yet she warned her daughter to be quiet.

"She doesn't mean the letter?" whispered Jermyn.

"Alas, no!" sighed Trif. "How I wish it might be!"

# CHAPTER XXVIII.
## THAT SURPRISE.

THE dinner was all that Trif had promised, and the guests were in high spirits, although some of them had believed in advance that it would be almost like a funeral feast, for were there not two blocks of stock which would not go out of the minds of at least two of the party?

Good manners prevented any show of sadness, and good company soon did the rest. There was an abundance of merry chat, and the host and hostess, with Harry and Fenie, encouraged the Admiral and Jermyn to tell stories of field and flood, of which civilians seem never to tire, so it was not until late in the evening that the party arose from the table. Then the ladies were begged for music, and the officers were coaxed to sing, and time flew so rapidly that it was almost midnight when the guests said they must take their leave, and Trif murmured that Trixy ought to have been put to bed hours before, but the dear child had been so quiet that her mother had scarcely known she was present.

"I dislike to bring up unpleasant subjects on such an occasion," said Phil, "but before we separate I must express my great sorrow and mortification at the loss of those pictures. I never before had so serious an accident, and I wish it were in my power to make some reparation."

"There is one way in which you can do it, my dear sir," replied the Admiral.

"What? Do name it and it shall be done."

"It is merely this. Kindly persuade your wife to re-write, from memory, and on the same kind of paper, if possible, the letter which, through my stupidity, has caused all the trouble. Have her write it with the same kind of ink; then give the letter to me!"

"I'll do it at once," said Trif.

"And you'll show me the letter?" added Kate.

"Not for worlds!" answered Trif, with a laugh and a blush that made Kate still more curious.

"What then?" asked Phil.

"Then," said the Admiral, firmly, "I shall duplicate my pencil sketch upon the back of it; Jermyn shall duplicate his on the back of the written page, and I shall file both as vouchers."

"A most brilliant plan!" exclaimed Phil. "Eh, Jermyn?"

"Brilliant enough," was the reply, "but I don't entirely like it. My friend, the Admiral, is the most honest man alive, yet to me the plan seems very like forgery."

"Oh, not at all!" said Phil. "A man can't forge his own writing or drawing. Besides, there's no question of morals involved. The company is willing to give the stock, in payment for services rendered, the services made by you gentlemen, showing how to get water to property which would be worthless without it. No other man, should he find the originals, can possibly present them or use them in any way, for he would not know what they signified, nor could he find any one but the existing company who could apply them to the property in question. Neither of you have talked of the matter elsewhere?"

"I don't believe," said the Admiral, with a long sigh, a shake of the head, and a reminiscent wink at Jermyn, "that any matter which affected business has ever been kept close by two men—eh, Jermyn?"

"Quite right, Admiral. Still, as to duplicating my sketch———"

"You can't prevent me, at least," the Admiral replied, "so I shall beg Mrs. Highwood to re-write the letter at once. If Jermyn chooses to throw away fifty thousand dollars—oh, Miss Trewman, you have more influence over him than any one else; do reason with him. Better still, command him. Don't let him throw good money to the dogs."

"What dogs? Who's throwin' money to 'em?" drawled Trixy, who had begun to fall asleep.

"Mr. Jermyn, my dear, is doing it," said Phil, "and all because your own father stupidly lost a couple of pictures."

"Gracious!" exclaimed the child, yawning and rubbing her eyes.

"What shall I do, my dear?" asked Jermyn, as Kate turned an anxious face toward him. "The money, should I get it, will be practically yours; that is, it will enable me to support my wife far better than my unaided salary will."

The Admiral, Fenie and Harry looked intently at Kate. Trif, at a table in the sitting room, had been writing rapidly with her husband looking over her shoulder. When she had finished Phil took the pen and did something to the letter, at which Trif nodded approvingly and then slyly drew Phil's face down to her and kissed it. Then she tore the two leaves of the sheet apart, and gave one to each of the despoiled men, saying,

"Admiral, this is the portion which you used. Jermyn, this is yours. Kate, have you brought him to his senses?"

"Shall I?" asked Jermyn.

"Yes," said Kate, "if you think it right."

"But I don't."

"Then you shan't" exclaimed Kate, snatching the paper from him. "No one shall ever blame you, though, for 'tisn't you who are throwing away the money; it is I."

She stepped quickly toward the grate, extended her hand, stopped, turned her head and said:

"As some reward for my self-sacrifice, mayn't I read the letter before I burn it?"

"You poor child!" murmured Trif.

"What? Was it as bad as that?"

"Look at it, Kate," said Phil, "and you will know what Trif means."

In a second Kate was under the chandelier and turning the sheet, but as she looked her face became blank, for Phil, supposing the paper was to go into the hands of a lot of business men, had penned over every line so skillfully, after the manner of commercial correspondents who make erasures in letters, that not a word of the original writing was decipherable.

"You shall know it all, you dear disappointed girl," said Trif. "I shall tell you every word of it this very evening—this very moment. Come with me; I know the others will excuse us under the circumstances."

Together they started to leave the room, but encountered Trixy, who was just entering.

"I most forgot about that s'prise," said the child to Jermyn, as she stopped before him. "The dinner was so good, and you folks talked so much, that I didn't get a chance to say nothin', and then I got sleepy while you was singin', and I'd have forgot all about it entirely if you hadn't begun to talk about throwin' money to dogs, and papa explained how it was."

Then she raised both hands high in the air and shouted:

"Here's your old pictures."

"Come on, boys," shouted the Admiral, springing forward, and snatching both sketches. He explained afterward, very sheepishly, that he believed his mind had been weakened by long anxiety about those sketches, for he imagined himself young again, and taking part in a landing party in Mexico.

"Oh, Trixy," exclaimed Trif, snatching her child into her arms, "you naughty, precious, dreadful, blessed, awful, angelic, terrible, lovely darling!"

"Jermyn!" exclaimed Kate, and Jermyn opened his arms, while Fenie gasped "Harry!" and Harry made haste to support her. The ladies being thus disposed of, the Admiral and Phil could only shake hands, which they did with a vigor that made each man wince. Finally Phil said:

"My dear, will you kindly stop kissing that child long enough for me to ask her a question? Trixy, where did you get those sketches?"

"Why, I found out that 'twas you that took one of 'em out of my scrap-book, and I thought it was just one of your tricks, so I'd play one on you, and the first thing I knew I got the chance, 'cause a lot of papers fell out of a coat of yours on a chair, and there was one of the pictures on the outside of a letter, and 'twas my own picture, so I took it, and afterwards I found there was one somethin' like it on the inside part of the letter, and I was goin' to tell you, some time, how nicely I had tricked you. Then I heard a lot of talk about pictures that the Admiral and Mr. Jermyn wanted, and I thought mebbe I had 'em, and I knew mamma was goin' to have both of the gentlemen here to dinner in a day or two, and I thought I'd keep the s'prise till then, when there'd be more people to laugh at it."

"Suppose," said Trif with frightened eyes, "that I had set the dinner for to-morrow instead of to-day!"

"But you didn't, my dear madam," said the Admiral. "All the world loves a lover, and I devoutly believe heaven does too. Suppose that you had put Trixy to bed at the usual hour!"

"Oh, don't!"

"Let me see the sketches, Admiral," said Kate. She looked at them carelessly, turned them over, and said:

"Trif, the writing on this page has been erased. May I read it?"

"Yes, dear, if you will take it into the next room."

Kate was absent several moments—a long time, Jermyn said, to read what his own eyes had seen at a glance, but when she returned she embraced Trif effusively and Jermyn told himself that Kate's eyes were most angelic when they were dewy.

---

There was a double wedding in June, and the Admiral, by permission of both families, gave away both brides. Trixy strewed flowers in front of each couple as they walked up the aisle of the church, and she looked and felt as important as if she were both brides. Neither couple asked her to be their guest on their wedding journey, which she thought rather strange, in view of their extreme affection for her, and her mother had much difficulty in explaining. Both brides, however, had her visit them soon afterward, and for so long a time that Trif began to complain that she had no daughter.

Milton Keynes UK
Ingram Content Group UK Ltd.
UKHW030741071024
449371UK00006B/668